Sisters of the Golden Mountain

A Shamanic Initiation Into Fire

Margaret West

Blessed journey Nancy
love
Margaret!

Sisters of the Golden Mountain

Dedication

This book is dedicated to Mary Magdalene, Master Morya, and Helena Roerich. I am ever grateful for your continuing truth and wisdom. I also express gratitude to Russia and the Russian people for making this amazing journey possible.

Acknowledgements

This story of my journey in Russia is as accurate as my memory allows, except in some minor instances where the privacy of individuals or places has been protected. I express thanks to the many individuals I have met along the way.

Special thanks and gratitude to Kalindi Adamus for her persistent and untiring assistance in helping me with *Sisters of the Golden Mountain: A Shamanic Initiation Into Fire*. Heartfelt thanks to Pauline Lawson for the cover artwork. I also thank Judy Tait for her artwork in the epilogue depicting the Altai Sisters. Other special mentions in Canada include Natania Winegrave, the Grace Society, and Ray McNally. Thanks and appreciation also to Lulu and Smashwords.

In Russia, I extend my thanks to all camp leaders and organizers of the Perm region, as well as Anna Aydarova and her large group of interpreters. I extend thanks and special mention for Galina Irmolina, Marina Tyasto, and Sveta Kameneva.

Internationally, a special thanks goes to Carol Bruce in the UK who first made it possible for me to travel to Russia. Special thanks also to Jan Secor, USA, as well as Mary Fisher in India and the Community of Gobin Sadan.

Special acknowledgement of Ludmilla Shaposhnikova, of the International Center of the Roerichs, Moscow, and Alena Adamkova, Curator of the International Roerich Memorial Trust, Kulla, India. Special thanks also to Daniel Entin, Director of the Nicholas Roerich Museum, New York, for his research assistance and his generosity.

Finally, I thank Nadia Vedernikova for the sharing of her prophetic dream – may we all continue to cooperate from a listening heart. I thank all for your continued encouragement.

Ho!

Contents

Acknowledgements   i

Map of Russia   v

Foreword   vii

Introduction – The Journey   1

Chapter 1 – The Calling   5

Chapter 2 – Arrival in Russia   11

Chapter 3 – Stepping into the Sacred   17

Chapter 4 – Cornerstones of the Journey   27

Chapter 5 – Gift of Humility   37

Chapter 6 – Dreams and Prophecies   46

Chapter 7 – A Journey within the Journey   53

Chapter 8 – The Mother of the World   67

Chapter 9 – Circles, Celebration and Healing   75

Chapter 10 – The Shift   86

Chapter 11 – Blessed by the Elementals   93

Chapter 12 – The Test   104

Chapter 13 – Mask Making   117

Chapter 14 – Connection to the Land   123

Chapter 15 – Visiting the Shamans   132

Chapter 16 – Meeting the Elder with Heart   142

Chapter 17 – Past and Present – Maria and the Ice Princess   151

Chapter 18 – Miracle of the Red Rose   159

Chapter 19 – Travelling to Eden   171

Chapter 20 – Coming Full Circle   182

Chapter 21 – Reclaiming the Feminine Principle   190

Chapter 22 – Message in the Sword   199

Chapter 23 – Kindello, the Full Round   211

Chapter 24 – Destiny   221

Epilogue   228

Appendix   233

Notes   237

Textual Sources   243

Map of Russia

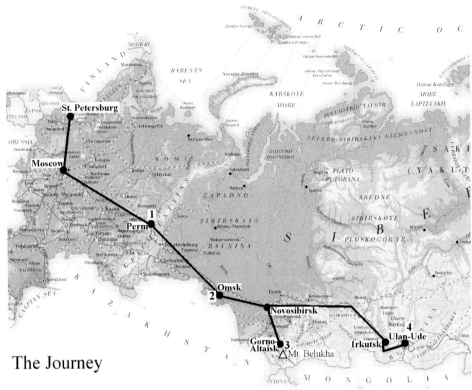

The Journey

1. Perm Region (Urals)
   - Family Camps
   - Cherdon
   - Mylobka
   - Point of Connection
   - Solikamsk

2. Omsk Region
   - Okunyova (Ashram)

3. Gorno-Altaisk Region (Altai)
   - Lake Teletskoe
   - Mt. Belukha
   - Artybash
   - Ust Khan (Maria)
   - Mendur Sakkon
   - Chendek
   - Uimon
   - Field of Babas
   - Kauri (Aktru)

4. Lake Baikal Region
   - Alhon Island
   - Shaman`s Rock

Foreword

Beginning a new journey

Joining:

We come to the joining of heaven and Earth
To the joining of Earth and of sky
To the joining of oceans and streams of the Earth
To the joining of East and of West, by and by.
Ho! M.W.

An old Grandmother sat alone on top of the tor. She had come to pray, just as she had each morning for twenty-one days; praying for connection to global community. Deep in her bones she knew a new journey was aching to begin. Prayers complete, she began to make her way back down the hill. Suddenly, a small brown rabbit hopped onto her path, escorting her back down the hill.

The hare, or rabbit, in England is the symbol for the Goddess Andraste. Some believe she is the bringer of wisdom for a new time. She is the keeper of truth and justice. Despite her gentle medicine, she possesses a fierceness that encapsulates truth and justice for all.

What then would this new journey look like – a journey destined to reach across nations, boundaries, and races; a vision that would connect communities in a simple way. Ordinary people merely dressed in the sacred. What form would that take, and how? Deep down a glimmer of stirring was beginning. From deep within, Grandmother knew. *"To behold the eyes of heart, to listen with the ears of heart to the roar of the world: to peer into the future with the comprehension of heart, thus must one impetuously advance on the path of ascent."* (1)

Let the journey begin! Ho!

Introduction – The Journey

First trip to Russia, 1995

Each step a journey, each journey a step

The sacred landscape there anew

Forever changing, not forgotten. M.W.

1

The Shamanic journey is life changing. It is similar to the hero's journey, where one is taken through intensive preparation, through a time of feeling totally alone, and then launched on the journey itself in search of a higher truth (1). Simply put, the journey is always a cycle: departure, fulfillment and return.

Two characteristics specific to the Shamanic journey, however, is first a deeply profound connection to the Earth; many of the teachings are hidden there and without this connection to the land would be missed. The second characteristic is the building of a solid foundation based on the old traditions. Movement of the journey stems from the concept that to move forward we must first move back, gleaning wisdom from the ancestors. The journey is a quest, a search, almost like a treasure hunt, and the clues of the hunt are set out somewhat like footprints in the earth. These clues are repeated sometimes gently, at other times more harshly, until the student is able to absorb the teachings and integrate them at a cellular level.

Shamanism, being universal, is practiced throughout the world, evolving from ancient traditions. It is also experiential in nature. At this physical level all senses of the student are brought into play, often at a heightened level. It is a visceral experience.

As part of the journey animals or birds will come to the student, sometimes in dream, but more often in the physical form. In Shamanic terms these helpers are called totems or power animals. They are there to enhance the teachings, helping us to become more aware. One of the first goals is to pay attention, to really *see* what is being presented. We have to be conscious on different levels of what is present there in the silence. Earth's creatures help us do this. They are also there to protect and support the student.

As the journey evolves the student is also taught through dreams. Shamanic dreaming is different from our ordinary dreaming in that the dreams are totally lucid. There is clarity of detail, including brightness of colors, sometimes complete with sound, action, and even smell, though this is rare. Upon awakening the student then has total recall of the dream and that memory stays with the student, always present to help with the teaching.

In my earlier training I was introduced to teachings around the medicine wheel. In these teachings the student learns all aspects of each direction, eventually able to live in balance from all four directions. The novice is then taken to a deeper level, to the elements associated with each of the four directions, which include earth, water, air, and fire. They are expected to become proficient in working with each of the elements and the lessons therein. In the lessons of the earth for example, one was taught to be grounded, to be connected to "one," whereas the lessons of water represented lessons of the feminine. These levels are sequential and usually take several years to complete.

I was now moving into a new area – one of fire. I had glimpsed a small snapshot of this element very early on. It was when I was preparing to attend a large gathering with Lynn Andrews. At the gathering they were setting up a world altar and had invited participants to bring something for the altar. For this purpose I had made a talking stick and then asked members of the groups I was then working with to add their prayers to the stick. One evening, prior to the beginning of group, I placed the talking stick on a large red cloth, planning to then put it in the center of the circle. Suddenly, without warning, the cloth and the stick burst into flames. When the fire was extinguished the cloth was badly seared, but the stick remained intact. This early introduction to the element of fire taught me first to respect such a potent element, but more it made me realize that there was a powerful teaching about fire hidden within the mystery of prayer and the sacred.

A journey is tailor-made by the cosmos but also uniquely formed to fit the characteristics of the individual. Quite marvelous when you think about it! There are, however, basic steps which tend to be common for all seekers and usually culminate in an initiation. This journey, my subsequent initiation into fire, would be no exception. So where would this journey take me and what would be the lessons along the way?

On the outer edges of my "knowing" the call was about to come. Ho!

Chapter 1 – The Calling

Ancient Shaman's Drum
Museum of Gorny Altaisk, Siberia

Come sisters of heart, come brothers of heart

Come journey to cast a new flame

It's a journey of hope, a journey of vision

A journey of peace we can dream. M.W.

The Lesson:

The journey usually begins with a calling, a tug into the non-ordinary reality. Shamanic tradition has a quality of mysticism that transports the individual into a dramatic link with spirit. This link then etches the experience into the initiate's psyche. This event is usually experienced within nature.

I had moved recently to a tiny secluded island – one that still possessed the potency of primal nature. It was here that I would later return after my trips to Russia, to give myself time to integrate the experiences. Here the hidden meanings of each journey would be flushed out, helping me to understand.

The beginning of a new journey is preceded by the death of the old one. The calling, often a sudden mysterious experience, is usually instigated by a Shamanic death, thrusting the initiate forward into the teachings of a new level. The death, often accompanied by visions and dreams, is very physical and not easy. The old level literally dies into the new lessons. This new level of teaching can take months, sometimes years, depending on the readiness of the initiate and the timing of spirit.

This time the call came with the drum. The exquisite sound of Mother Earth's heartbeat, as mirrored in the drum, helps us connect to the Earth beneath our feet and reminds us that we are truly connected to all living things. With the closing of one millennium and the dawning of the new, it was not surprising the call of the drum rang out, calling me to a new journey. So the journey began, going to bed one night. It was a very ordinary night, so common one almost missed it. Under the layer of ordinary, however, came the call to the new teaching – a journey of both challenge and mystery.

I had heard the drums beating all night long. The constant sound became waves that resonated with the rhythm of my sleep patterns, caught in the magic of the dream. Calling, pulsing, drumming, yet always clearing the path to remembrance. It was very old, this call, seeming to come from deep within the womb of the Earth. A calling from the ancient ancestors. Calling to come, a pulse so deep that I had almost forgotten.

There, in my tiny Northern cabin, just as I was drifting off to sleep the call persisted; the deep, resonate sounds of many, many drums; drums of the ancestors calling throughout the night with their primal, earthy song. I would ease into slumber only to be roused once again by their call. It was like a tug to remember – remembering a birthright that had belonged to us for centuries. It was calling us to awaken and remember the Sacred Flame.

It was so old and distant, tattered and worn, yet still remained, awaiting the moment of rebirth. It was a call to wisdom – that instinctual knowledge that was so often scorned. Despite the relentless push to stay in fear, the call of the drum was stronger.

Miraculously the flame was still alive. Its deep glowing embers cast into the murky caverns of lost dreams, still awaiting the tiniest breath of air that would come to fan this sacred memory.

This memory, the memory of the flame, had once been fierce and strong. Now it stood silent and alone, lifeless without connection to the past. Now only a mere specter of its vibrant past. Within the resounding vibration of the drum I was pushed back to the ancient days when there were priestesses who guarded the flame, caretakers of the sacred. These Ancients had been guardians of holy wisdom. The call, the dream, always felt very ancient; a pulling down to the watery depths of Atlantis, yet seeming older still. As the drums continued beating out the message of this, our sacred heritage, the message was simple. Each of us holds this precious resonance of our Mother's heartbeat.

The message of the Ancients told me it was time; time to reclaim a birthright so long discarded and forgotten; time to remember that we as sisters share that pulse as ancient as the beat of our Mother's heart. It was time to remember who we really are, reclaiming wisdom through the flame of connection to each and every living being on the planet.

Yes, from the profound silence came the deep continuous beat of the drum, broken only by the gentle lapping of the oceans waves, coming from the collective voices of the ancestors, pulsing across the ethers to caress the tattered edges of our souls – each of us suffering in our own way from acute spiritual starvation. The call to wisdom echoed on the fire of the drumbeat, echoing on the mist again and again, the message so simple in the call. I was being called to remember myself as a sister, a keeper of the sacred; a call for all to remember we are daughters of this planet. It came in the form of a sister's song.

<u>Sisters of the Earth:</u>

Sisters of the Earth are calling to you
Sisters of the Earth are crying for you
Sisters of the Earth are claiming for you
This Mother we call home.

We honor the ones behind us
We honor the ones before us
The stars above and the Earth below
Calling all sisters home.

We are weaving our quilt of stories
Weaving the colors together
And the quilt will girdle the planet
For our Mother we call home.

Each patch holds love and beauty
Each square a heart told story
A garden of truth and beauty
Calling all sisters home.

Sisters of the Earth are calling to you
Sisters of the Earth are crying for you
Sisters of the Earth are claiming for you
Our Mother we call home.

Ho!

Chapter 2 – Arrival in Russia

First trip to Russia, 1995

Top left: St. Petersburg

*Top right: Sacred spring,
Lake Teletskoe area*

*Left: Conference in
Novosibirsk, Siberia*

Where East is East and West is West
And never the twain shall meet. M.W.

The Lesson:

Prior to any journey there is a period of time when you experience a
disquieting shift in your energy. Old ways and conditioning seem to
slough off, almost like a snake shedding its skin. Everything around

and inside one slows down; you feel disconnected, especially to spirit. In the creative process it is often called "the dark night of the soul." Within Shamanic reference it is death, often accompanied by a dream of dismemberment – of being broken apart only to be reassembled. This is the universal process known as death, birth, and transformation. With death the new setting is revealed.

I have often thought our guidance in the cosmos has a profound sense of humor. My invitation for my first trip to Russia came from the Spaceclub. My friend Carol from Glastonbury, England, who had previously travelled in Russia, was inviting me to an international conference that was to be held in Siberia. I had previously met Carol in Glastonbury. This wise-woman, often described as "larger than life," shared my love and strong connection to Russia. One of the many staunch light workers of the planet, she would later travel with me to various places in Russia including Lake Teletskoe and Perm, helping my journey unfold.

The conference was sponsored by the cosmonauts and it was to focus on "The Cosmos and Man." It would include a dialogue on socio-economic problems facing mankind. Within this context was a question: What is woman's role in the ongoing dialogue with spirit?

To travel in Russia I needed an invitation, which was then submitted to the Russian Consulate to receive a visa. During this early period of collapse, prior to email, it was not uncommon for phones and

12

faxes to crash. This, coupled with our challenging language barriers, made it a small miracle that we were able to get to Russia that first time.

Nothing prepared me for what I would witness upon my arrival in Moscow. The onset of the journey took me to Russia at a most unusual time. Beset with serious economic problems, Russia was trying desperately to rebuild. In 1985, Gorbachev inaugurated the new strategy of Perestroika (1). It was hoped that this return to basics would help the country break through serious economic inertia and stagnation. Although this vast nation had been able to bring itself out of the tatters and ruin of World War II, this time it was unable to succeed in doing so. The economy had collapsed. Stark poverty pervaded everywhere. Moscow was cold, gray, and bleak, much like the blanket of despair that covered all life in the city. Grandmothers were begging on the streets. Everything seemed harsh and extreme. At night the Red Square was virtually deserted.

A young woman who was helping us as an interpreter used an intriguing metaphor to describe the conditions at that time (I would later discover that her work as our interpreter supported herself, her parents and her siblings). She said that the Iron Curtain had been closed for so many years, that when it finally lifted a lot of dust and debris had to be blown away to reveal the real jewel of Russia.

The monetary system too had collapsed. Those that may have had meager savings watched helplessly as over night their savings vanished. People were not being paid and goods and services were not available. Just to survive people had to turn once more to the land, to their dachas (gardens), and to what they could forage in the forests just to get enough food to sustain themselves. I remember later on during that first trip, going into a local store in a tiny village that was close to the Mongolian border. The inventory consisted of one jacket, one pair of shoes, and a small amount of sugar. Nothing else – no medicine, just what had been produced locally. Conditions were indeed desperate.

In witnessing this harsh erosion of a proud nation, I too began to experience a breaking down of my own inner plane. Soon there was a deterioration of previous beliefs and prejudices, a sloughing off of old propaganda which had been fed to me in my Western world since childhood. Just perhaps, a new perception was about to emerge.

Yet despite these tragic conditions of no food, no money, no goods or services, our Russian hosts were there to share with us whatever they had. They hosted us with enthusiasm, excitement, and often humor. Most folks I would meet possessed what I would come to call the indomitable Russian spirit. They somehow had the ability to deal with huge difficulties on a daily basis, obstacles that they had overcome throughout their harsh, ancient history. I was continually amazed by their strength and their warmth. I also sensed a deep integrity with all those I encountered.

This was demonstrated by a young man, an armed guard, while we were getting our money changed. In those early days there were no banks as such. Instead, we were taken to the back of a building and each of us in turn was directed into a small room. Upon entering the room we were asked to be seated on the one single chair to carry out our transaction. Two armed guards would stand on either side watching the proceedings. Not prepared for these, the armed companions, it was easy to conjure up negative impressions.

Once back at the hotel one of our group, to her dismay, discovered she had left her wallet with the remainder of her American money behind at the money changers. Just then, a knock came at the door. Standing outside was the armed guard with our friend's wallet in his hand. It seems he had noticed the wallet shortly after we had left and had rushed to follow us all the way back to the hotel, returning it to the lady whom had left it behind. Things were not always as they seemed. This was a phrase that would repeat itself over and over on my future travels.

Who were these courageous people who lived continuously with such paradox? What was it that gave them their indomitable spirit, their strength, their stamina? Despite daily struggle they also appeared to possess a strong vision for the future.

I met a beautiful young woman whose name was Nadya. This slim, blond, blue-eyed woman with a gentle soul shared with me her dream. Somewhat prophetic of the journey, in her dream she saw many, many women of the world coming together as sisters, making a long, long girdle which encircled the planet. She saw herself there with her daughter. She saw me, along with many, many sisters, all participating in ceremony; linking like a sister belt around our Mother – Mother Earth. Women sang beautiful songs; we danced and expressed much joy. Nadya believes dreams are "real," and she said, "To tell you the truth, I want to make this a reality – to create this belt that will become a vibrant, living banner."

Transiting this mysterious and beautiful land, preparations for the first steps of the journey would begin. At the end of the conference I would receive the first clue that would begin to reveal the mystery.

Let the journey continue! Ho!

Chapter 3 – Stepping into the Sacred

Ancient rosary gifted to author, 1995

The chalice, the stone, hidden symbols of wisdom
Their flame like a fiery new sword. M.W.

The Lesson:

When setting out on a journey, one must move into a particular
mindset to ready oneself for the teachings. This mindset is described
as reverence. Reverence is defined as having deep respect mingled
with wonder. Rather than worship, it is a state of being where one

honors all life around them. It is then, and only then, that the teachings of the journey will begin to reveal themselves.

When I first arrived in Russia, I would witness time and again the deep reverence that was demonstrated by people in the many ancient churches. It was not uncommon to see grandmothers prostrate before a Mary Icon. I remember being taken to a museum where one whole floor was dedicated to the ancient Icons, many seeming to symbolize the "Sophia" – Mary, but with white hair and robes of brilliant scarlet. These ancient paintings were powerful enough to move one to tears.

What made up this mysterious country and Her people? How could they live day to day with little food and (if working) no pay, yet share whatever they had and continue to shine with the radiance of an old soul? I began to realize that there was a Russia that many Westerners, myself included, had no inkling of – a Russia of deep faith and mystery. This Russia was rich with an ancient heritage; one that had an ongoing connection to a plethora of spiritual traditions. These traditions, ranging from the original Shamanic traditions (still very much alive today), going even further back to Vedic teachings, and back even further to the time of the Scynthians. A rich heritage of the sacred clothed in magic and mystery, and it was one of Russia's best kept secrets. Unlike the usual trip to the various tourist destinations I somehow curiously fell between the cracks into a very different Russia. I had landed at the grassroots level and soon friends were sharing many things. It was from this perspective that I began to appreciate my surroundings.

They told me of an area outside of Perm, where legend had it that at one time Roshis lived. There was also rich tribal wisdom in the area, including that of a tribe called the Mansi. Outside the Omsk area a friend who ran an ashram dedicated to Baba Ji found a stone bust of Hanuman in the woods. Folklore of this area spoke of a hidden city buried under the lake. In Siberia, in the Altai the Elders still remember the Holy Ones that lived in the nearby mountains that came to teach the people.

Coming from this deep foundation of traditions it is not uncommon for people to practice a synthesis of traditions. A friend in Perm, for example, who followed the Christian faith, was also very interested in Shamanic healing practices and would go regularly to the village wise-woman to get herbs to cleanse her home.

My first introduction to this ancient spiritual heritage came in the form of a gift. In making my presentation at the conference I followed the theme of "woman's role in the dialogue with spirit," presenting my poem – a prayer to Mary Magdalene.

Magdalene

Ah Magdalene, vine of life
Yours is a lusty passion that makes all things grow.
That instinctual aliveness we have all forgotten.

How beautiful you are!

Coming to me through the mist
Coming to all with so much love.

Twin towers of faith, steady as the Ancient Ones themselves
My Ave Maria, my Sophia, my Crone.

Taking the trail of tears and lifting it to spirit
Come to me my Sophia, my beloved.

Invoke in me the courage and the strength needed for the
        task at hand
Part the mist and scatter the raindrops upon the parched
        wasteland of denial
Creating the green mountain of the sacred world
The alive, pregnant mountain of a New Jerusalem.

I call to you Wise-woman, my beloved Magdala.
Yours is the wisdom so longed for to open our hearts.

Do you hear this humble cry to my star child Maria?
Do you hear the call for the gift of the muses?

Ah Maria, my vine of life
Weaving a wholeness for this illumined pathway
Mystical tapestry, a weaving of heaven on Earth.

Behold the New Jerusalem, giver of life to the humble and the meek
Giver of life of the crystal web
Mighty Earth Priestess that you are, bring the magic words
and help them flow
Flow like the turbulent river of knowledge
Flow like the gentle river of wisdom
Merger of red and white springs of truth
Alchemy of love bringing this Tree of Life.

Thank you, my beloved Maria, for hearing this humble prayer.
Blessed be the trinity of the feminine.
Blessings for Mother Mary, Blessings be for Magdala.
Blessed be to the Mother Of Us All.

Blessed be, Blessed be, Ave Maria, Ave Maria,
Our Magdala, our truth, our bloom.

And so it is, above, below and all around.

Ho! M.W.

I was startled by the response. Many in the audience were crying.
Some were raising their hands in affirmation – a poignant outpouring
of reverence. Keep in mind that Russian people were coming from
seventy years of being forbidden to express their spirituality openly.
They had to be inward where they held on tenaciously to a deep

21

faith. A friend of mine described how she would sneak off from time to time to her mother's remote village to attend church. She did this at great risk to herself and her family. Her husband being quite high up in the political party of the time meant that both she and her husband could have lost their jobs – could have in fact been blacklisted.

The next day I discovered a gift had been left for me. The gift was similar to a necklace, with round circles of leather pieced together, joined at the bottom by two pieces of suede that were in the shape of a Christmas tree. What I would not realize until much later was that I had been given a rosary. In later doing research I discovered that it was similar to the first rosaries ever made; these ancient rosaries contained a prayer in each of the leather rounds. A special gift indeed! It became like a sacred link pushing me forward on my journey. It seems my prayer to Mary had been powerfully answered.

During the course of my decade-long journey I would go to Russia eight times for a total of thirty-three weeks. During that span of time I spent only three nights at a hotel. The rest of the time I was home-stayed. The rosary acted as a covenant as my friends now became determined to show me what they referred to as the "real Russia." It became a mystical journey without political agenda or mistrust. The Russian people began to share their mystical, ancient heritage, their traditions and folklore, as well as the beauty of Mother Russia Herself. This, in their hearts, was the real Russia, the one so instinctively intertwined with their own souls.

Now, as my journey progressed, more traditions would unfold. In Perm I would see exhibits that displayed artifacts of the Chudd. These were animal style figures that dated from the 8th–13th century. These figures were originally totems and represented animal ancestors that were revered by the ancient peoples. This type of art – animal, sometimes part animal and part human – had been found in the Perm region, as well as Western Siberia. Christianity eventually brought an end to this art, but remnants of the style remain evident in folk art today. (1)

In the Lake Baikal region, Shamanic traditions were predominately followed in the North, whereas in the South there was a mix of both Shamanic and Buddhist traditions. The central Buddhist temple was just outside Ulan Ude. The Buddhist faith had flourished in the early days, but during the revolution some two hundred and fifty temples were destroyed. Now they were again rebuilding. While visiting the temple we were able to speak briefly to the Lama there. He showed us some of the ancient texts that they had managed to preserve, like the teachings of the Blue Buddha. No one knew how old these precious texts were. While in the area we also visited a women's Buddhist monastery. The young nuns residing there, devotees of Tara and Buddha, worked during the day, held their daily services, and still had time to counsel and heal within the inner city community.

I would meet several from a group called the Old Believers. This was a group who, nearly three centuries before, had split from the

Orthodox Christian church in what became known as the Great Schism. Old Believers had objected both to changes in the prayer book as well as significant changes to the ritual of the service. This group were severely persecuted, but rather than submit to the imposed new ways, chose instead to hide away in remote areas of Russia.

The Altai was one such place, and while travelling on Lake Teletskoe we stopped at a research station where we were introduced to a woodcutter who had been in their service for over forty years. He was a friend of one such family, known in the West as the Lykovs (2). The last word we as Westerners had heard was that all of the family had died with the exception of the daughter Agafia. The woodsman told us that Agafia still lived hidden away but had now been joined by others to form a community and they were still practicing their ancient faith. This rich and diverse heritage called the "real Russia" became the fabric which appeared to influence the makeup of the Russian people. It also became the mosaic from which my journey was etched.

As early as the 1980s, a new source of spirituality emerged in Russia known as *The Teachings of Agni Yoga* or sometimes called *The Living Ethics*. At first, small bits of The Teachings were smuggled into Russia. Curiously, the border guards never detected these copies. As my friend Galina explained, during the time of Communism in Russia it was very difficult to get esoteric books to read, especially anything outside of Russia. Most churches were silent. Helena Roerich wrote thirteen volumes called *The Teachings of Agni Yoga*. She was guided by the Mahatmas, also known as The Lords of Wisdom or Lords of Shambhala, who were a group of enlightened beings that have chosen to assist mankind with their evolution here on Earth (3). Ultimately these teachings spread across Russia and became, as one friend described, a flood of new knowledge.

In a quote from Harold Balyoz's book, *Three Remarkable Women*: *"Yet, inspired by Master Morya... Helena Roerich brought us the teachings of Agni Yoga, the highest form of yoga. The Agni Yoga books, in thirteen slim volumes, carry no author's credit line in them, although they contain, without a doubt, the most advanced spiritual philosophy ever given to humanity."*(4) Today these teachings have spread throughout the world.

Written with a flavor of Sanskrit and Senzar, making it sometimes difficult to translate, it is considered the yoga of fire – Agni meaning fire and Yoga meaning connection to the highest (5). The central teachings focus was on the understanding of energy and fire, further stressing that we have a subtle body as well as a physical body; that we are all made up of energy and it is through prana (nature) that we nourish our life force. It is believed to be a synthesis of previous teachings.

Just as the Shamanic traditions focus on the elements, the Agni Yoga teachings encourage the student to become proficient at achieving mastery at the physical, astral, and fiery level. In Agni Yoga the heart is referred to as the chalice center, that subtle organ that links a person to their own spark of divinity, often referred to as their higher selves. The Teachings stress a better understanding of energy, but also help us comprehend wisdom and the ethics of living, ultimately promoting a great synthesis of all things. It is a teaching that encourages living in the heart.

Nicholas and Helena Roerich were a remarkable Russian couple (see appendix for complete history). Nicholas was a master painter and writer; Helena too was a writer. They had left Russia due to Nicholas' poor health just prior to the revolution. Sadly, they were never able to return, but never forgot their homeland, referring always to the New Country that would emerge in Russia. They worked tirelessly throughout their lives for the betterment of humanity, stressing always the importance of the role of the Feminine Principle and for peace, these themes expressed repeatedly in their writing. The Roerich's vision unfolded as a great banner – their dream of unity ultimately becoming the sacred circle of eternity as symbolized in the Roerich banner of peace.

These new Teachings would ultimately have a huge impact on both my journey and my initiation into fire. With the stage for the journey now set, I move deeper into the realms of the real Russia so more of the journey can be revealed.

May the journey continue. Ho!

Chapter 4 – Cornerstones of the Journey

Left: Aktru, Altai Region   Right: Master Throat Singer

As he swoops and he dives, air pockets his friends

Honor mighty dear eagle, your wish his command. M.W.

The Lesson:

With the setting of the journey in place, as well as the mindset established, the student is then provided with two cornerstones that are there to cradle the journey. The first is the appreciation and knowledge of the old traditions. We cannot separate the past from the future – to be able to move forward we must first go back. The second cornerstone is a profound connection to the land.

Shamanism in Russia is ancient – considered by some to be as old as humanity, depending on how strictly or loosely one defines the term. In my frame of reference I refer to those connected to the Earth in a spiritual way. The various practices in Siberia were largely left uninterrupted for centuries. This was due in part to the vastness of the region and how difficult it was to get there. It was a practice followed by both men and women – many of the myths attributing much power to the feminine, often describing the first Shaman as female (Shamanka). (1)

In Russia there is a delicate mysticism embedded in the Earth that enables the student to see at a deeper level. This profound interconnection of land and traditions gives the student not only a foundation, but also an impetus to the forward movement of the journey. This vital combination would be presented many times during my journey in Russia.

After the conference we made our way to the Altai. The Republic of the Altai lies in the South of Siberia. There is a special legend connected to the Altai border. Long, long ago, a great Babyrgan (lord) had a daughter called Katuny. She had fallen in love with the strong Bia, and the lovers made plans to escape. Her father was furious when he heard of the lovers plans and began to chase his daughter. He was not able to catch her as she ran away as a strong river to her beloved. The lovers met and formed one mighty river called Ob, meaning both. They are now together, on their continual journey flowing north. As for the father, because of his great rage the spirits turned him into the big mountain called Babyrgan. He sits motionless, time without end, guarding the border of Gorny-Altai on the banks of the Katun River. (2)

We travelled initially to the main town of Gorno-Altaisk. It was here, by chance, that we met the Throat Singer and he immediately agreed to sing for us. The Throat Singer's gift is one of the ancient traditions still honored today. The unique qualities of this gift are palpable on ones body – a powerful means of attaining balance and healing. As he sang it was like each of one's chakra centers were being cleared and balanced. I was fortunate to meet this gifted Shaman several times during my many visits to the Altai.

It is important to speak of this meeting with the Throat Singer. I wish to tell you of him because he is one of the Old Ones (Shamans) in the tradition that he follows; a tradition that may be a dying breed. I need to speak of the beauty of his gift; the beauty of healing sound, so exquisite that once it is heard one is never again quite the same.

The Throat Singer arrived early, as did I. He was a handsome man – perhaps in his late forties or older. He was wearing a white t-shirt with an eagle flying on the front of it. He had the high cheekbones and almond shaped eyes specific to his indigenous race. What stood out the most were his eyes; large liquid pools of sadness, framing the doorway to this man's beautiful soul. Although small in stature, his presence was large; a presence which emanated deep peace.

Soon people were arriving and the Throat Singer's presentation was about to begin. The music of throat singers is truly unique. It lies somewhere between the overtone chanting of the Tibetan monks and the Eskimo singers of the North. As he sang, the energy from his sound moved down to the very base of one's spine, deep into the Earth. It would then soar up to the very crown of your head. As one listened you could sense this healing vibration in your body and physically feel the clearing and cleansing of each chakra center. His songs were about animal totems, about Mother Russia, and about healing. Soon he was tired and asked if there were questions before ending his presentation. We would be joining him the next day when we did ceremony on the hill above Gorno-Altaisk.

Meanwhile, several of the women in Gorno-Altaisk had a dream. They wished to build a temple dedicated to Umai which would be a place of the synthesis of all world religions, as well as honoring indigenous traditions specific to the region. The cult of the ancient Turkic Goddess Umai had its beginnings sometime between 5 and 10 A.D. Also known as Mai–ene, she was the patron of women and children. At one time, somewhere near Teletskoe Lake in the Altai, there was a big stone which carried her image. She holds a small silver bow in her hands. According to legend, Belukha (the Altai sacred summit) is her domain. She is believed to be the Goddess of the Feminine Principle. During festivals devoted to the Goddess people decorate the birch tree; all things connected to the birch tree are considered sacred and thus revered (just as the cedar tree is for the Cosalish people in BC, Canada). For example, when a cradle for a new-born child was being made in the villages of Altai, the craftsman would try to behave in a good way and abstain from alcohol. While choosing the birch tree for the cradle the craftsman first prays to the spirits of place.

In the Altai there are very ancient traditions, but in recent years the people have tried to renew paganism, and at the beginning of the 20th century a new religion, Barchans', appeared. This religion holds the belief of the coming of their redeemer – the White Burkhan (God). *"On rock drawings in the Altai, one can see four birch trees said to be symbolic, which protect the place of birth."* It was out of this ancient mystery that the women of Gorno-Altaisk wished us to join them in a ceremony for their new temple, so we made our way up the hill to participate with them. The Throat Singer was also present and we acknowledged our connection by exchanging gifts.

Each participant was given a prayer tie to be placed on the nearby birch trees, tied on by each of us with our own special prayer. The placing of tie flags is a way of putting out prayer to spirit and communing with nature. After prayers were completed we formed a circle, the group organizer honoring Umai in the center with milk. A member from the UK set out a grid of crystals. The Throat Singer played a small string instrument and I drummed. What a fitting end to our conference.

Next morning our group was to travel into the Kourai Valley with Galina as our guide. Galina, whom I had met at the conference, acted as our group's interpreter. This slim, middle-aged woman with a fiery heart would form a staunch friendship with me over the coming years. Galina was a school teacher taking her training in Irsutsk, but she later married and then moved to Novosibirsk. As well as being a student of Agni Yoga, she also became fascinated with the Altai, drawn to this special land with its many legends and folktales. Galina eventually began to act as a guide and interpreter for visitors wishing to travel to the Altai. It was Galina who first introduced me to the teachings of Agni Yoga.

As we travelled, Galina shared a brief history abut the valley. It had once been a very busy trade route connecting to Mongolia and China. It was considered the old tea road. Now, being remote, most people had not encountered Westerners. My friend from England had been there once, and now with us travelling into the valley, it would be the second time they would meet Western women.

Kourai is considered a special spirit-filled place. This area has unique Baba stones which I would get to see later. The area also abounds with stories of spirits appearing among the people. One such story tells of a young man who was stopped by a young woman asking if she could ride with him on his motorcycle. He agreed and they drove off, the woman riding behind him. Upon arriving at a nearby settlement the driver was amazed to note that his passenger had vanished.

The only break on our long arduous journey had been a stop at a holy spring. We had pulled over to the side of the road and climbed out. There, on the side of the road amidst a cluster of rocks, cool pure water cascaded down, creating a mist of cool relief in the relentless Siberian summer heat. Framing the rocks were clusters of trees and upon the trees were tied many, many prayer ties. Fluttering slightly in the almost still summer breeze, they called their sacred welcome for all. There are many such stops along the remote roads of Siberia.

Soon we began making our descent into this low lying valley. The Altai Mountains were in the distance, casting shadows of deep violet in the dusky lateness of the day. As the sun skimmed the horizon, the sky began to change. Colors shifted from the blues of early day, to the pinks and vibrant oranges of dusk. Huge orange spirals swirled on the horizon, welcoming us to this remote village of Kourai. We had arrived!

Next day we would walk to a spring where the local people went to offer prayers. We were told that the people worshipped this place as the spirit of the mountains. As we approached, we were asked to proceed in respectful silence. It was a place where if people had recently lost loved ones they could go to honor the departed ones and release grief. When we arrived there was a family there from a nearby village. The eldest member of the family, a young woman, had brought her younger sister to the spring for a small ceremony. With Galina's help as interpreter, we were told that when children turned twelve they were presented with a shell on a string. It was given for protection and the child would wear it for a whole year. At the end of the year the children were given a new name, and then again when they reached twenty-four and thirty-six. At this spring they used offerings of either prayer ties or copper. We were told to hold up a copper penny, make a prayer, and then bend down and drink the water so as to fulfill our wish.

Meanwhile, plans were being made for a special expedition. The group, being large, was split into two groups. My group was to travel into the mountains. There had been heavy rain and some flooding, so we had to wait to see if the waters would begin to recede. Next morning it was deemed safe to proceed. We were all piled into a tractor drawn wagon. At many places the streams had swollen their banks, overflowing with rushing water. At each dangerous crossing the wife of the driver got out and did ceremony and prayer before we crossed the turbulent waters. She tied a prayer tie to a nearby tree. It was customary to do this, to honor the Spirits of Nature and ask for safe passage, just as it was customary to leave dishes of food for the dead ancestors.

Soon we were travelling along a high ridge of land that looked down at the raging river below, following a faint trail that etched its way

34

deeper into the mountains. As the landscape shifted it became alive with flowers. Pockets of tiny irises, a wild version of the peony (the Siberian flower), and many blooms from a variety of herbs all crowned the forest. Whole sides of hills were on fire with the fire bloom. It was magnificent to be walking with the Ancients.

Next morning Galina was to take us up to the glaciers located in the mountains called Aktru. Aktru means white place. Aktru Mountains are covered with eternal ice and snow. As we walked through the rounded boulders, ever upward, we came to a glacier fed lake tucked into the foot of the mountain. I waited here while the rest of the group hiked further upward.

I reveled in the silence, there beside the waters of the lake, drinking in the beauty of the mountain and the deep essence of the place. I began to notice perfect mirror images reflected in the water. Galina felt that this pristine place created a borderline between the two worlds. Locals called it a place where one can meet the Great Mountain Spirits and experience deep joy, here where the veil is thin. In this remote region I had been given a true example of "as above, so below."

Our group was silent as we returned to the little village of Kourai. I took this time to again reflect upon the lessons of the journey. The setting of the journey had placed me in Russia, where if I was able to step forward in both reverence and humility, unique teachings from the old traditions coupled with the potency of the land, then the lessons would continue to be revealed. Honoring the delicate interconnection of tradition and the power of the land, it paved the way for each forward step of the journey. I am full.

May the journey continue. Ho!

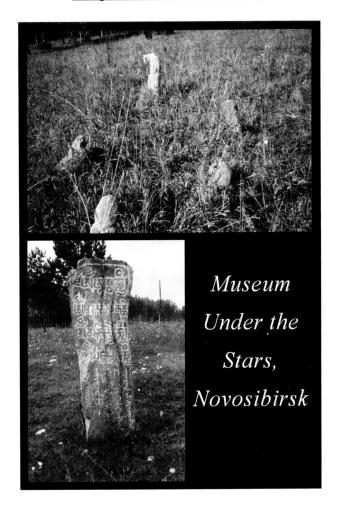

Museum Under the Stars, Novosibirsk

The ancestors, the Ancients, the ones of past glory

Through drumbeat, through heartbeat, they know of Earth's story.

M.W.

The Lesson:

As the journey proceeds and one is immersed in the ancient history of the land, one cannot but feel humble, realizing that there is much wisdom to be revealed. Once the trappings of the old story begin to fade away, the student – the pilgrim – can then tread the ancient land with respect and humility; small glimmerings of transformation begin to surface.

"They look at us in silence; some of them with a reproach and a hidden sadness; others with a playful smile screwing up their slanting eyes." (1)

Back again in Novosibirsk, plans were being made to see the Babas. It was a place called the Museum Under the Stars. The Museum Under the Stars houses a collection of Babas which had been found in the Altai. They are said to be Turkic in origin and are mostly male in this particular area, although the name Baba means grandmother in Russian. In some areas there are female figures. These intriguing stone sculptures date back more than one thousand years and are said to depict the warrior ancestors of that time. Often the figures are carved in full dress, complete with belts and daggers. Typically, the left hand of the figure is on their belt and the right hand holds a vessel or a cup. Many of them were found in the Southeastern part of the Altai and honor the ancestors. They were often erected close to stone enclosures, which seemed to serve not only as foundations for the stones but also as altars. To date, more than three hundred of the Baba stones have been documented (2). This unique legacy is not only a part of the Shamanic tradition, but dates back into antiquity to the Turks and the early Scythian times.

Three of us – Galina, my friend; Carolyn, a lady from the UK; and myself – would be going to see the Babas. In these early times taxis were not available. One had to go out on the road, flag down a car, and negotiate a ride. We arrived without incident at the gate, only to find it heavily padlocked and chained. Simultaneously, both Carolyn and I bowed our head in prayer. A moment later Carolyn reached up to touch the chain. The lock dropped away and the gate mysteriously swung open.

Inside the gate we found ourselves in a small field, but there appeared to be more stones further up where an old building was standing. As we looked more closely at the stones before us we were all deeply touched. Carolyn then went over to a flat stone which was edged with a petal-shaped carving, making it appear like a huge stone lotus. She felt drawn to do a ceremony there and called Galina to come and join her. There was ancient writing on a stone beside the lotus shaped altar. Some say the writing is older than Sanskrit, but no one really knows.

I decided to explore further up the field. As I got closer I looked over at the field where I saw dozens of the old Babas. Moving closer, I was overcome by emotion as I gazed upon these amazing old stones.

A field of Baba stones honoring the ancestors, standing there in silence; it was truly incredible! There were many, many stones, ranging from two to three feet in height, all standing silently before me. Some barely had a rough outline of a face carved into their surface while others were complete with beards and yet others had belts with what appeared to be a pouch attached; others seemed to be holding a cup in their hand.

I do not have words to describe the beauty of their old, craggy rock faces. They were the original grandmothers and grandfathers. I felt so honored to see them. Apparently a man had gathered up all these old stones, thinking that in so doing he would be bringing them to the people. He hoped to build a park where people could come to honor the Old Ones. Two years later, however, he died. Now, these Old Ones just stood there, separated from their place of origin. As I knelt there briefly, in this field of Old Ones, I felt so touched to experience this rare, preserved history. I also felt sadness. Just like so many Siberians, they too had been uprooted, ripped from the very root structure of their families and placed all alone in this empty field without the spirits of place or the landscape to comfort them. To be moved to a place where more could see, remember, honor, and perhaps protect this ancient heritage seemed like a huge sacrifice. Who is to say what the right way is.

Galina and Carolyn had moved over to a Baba that seemed to be off by itself. They called me to join them. This Baba was female and her face was clearly outlined in the stone. She appeared to be very old.

Her ancient arms were wrapped around a tall vase or jug. All three of us gazed into the craggy face of this old Ancient One. She radiated deep peace. Carolyn suggested we do a simple ceremony of connection with this incredible Old One. Holding hands we formed a small circle around the Baba stone; a woman from England, one from Siberia, and one from Canada all coming together to form a circle. East joined with West; a maid, a mother, a crone, bringing together our vision of peace, love, and healing for our beloved planet; three sisters standing in silence in that moment of the sacred, joining nations in simple communion. With our hands joined we each sent out our prayers in our own unique way; prayers for this Old One, prayers for our Mother Earth, for each nation, for all the children coming together as sisters and brothers in this special moment. Upon completion we looked up and smiled at each other, acknowledging what would forever be our special sister connection.

When I later described this ceremony to my friend in Glastonbury, she said that very likely the old Baba stone had been a symbol of Mother Earth. In her Romany traditions the vase symbolized the carrying of Her children which she cradled in Her arms.

Carol and I made our farewells to conference delegates. The profound impact of the Baba stones stayed with me as now Carol and I prepared to move on to the final leg of the journey. There was much to reflect upon as we travelled to the city of Omsk by train. It was referred to as a hidden city, meaning Westerners had not travelled there until recently.

The Siberian railway snaked persistently across the vast landscape of Siberia. Mile upon mile of meadows, trees, and water dotted the horizon as we moved once again westward. We pulled into the Omsk station and were met by Carol's friend. Despite the early hours of the morning these dedicated people were there to help us with our luggage and to greet us with a warm welcome. Carol's friend took us to his tiny village where we were to overnight and then leave the following morning on a trip further north to Okunyovo.

Next morning, we sat in the kitchen drinking tea while waiting for the bus to arrive. Gradually, other women from this tiny community came to join us. Despite their shyness we struggled to communicate. The Russian women suggested we could sing. In my decade-long journey in Russia music would always be a part of the journey, often filling the miles of travel plus helping bridge a tender connection. I believe one of the ways Russian people nourish their souls is to sing their favorite folk songs about Mother Russia (simple, yet hauntingly beautiful melodies about the land they so dearly love, despite countless hardships and struggle). By this time there were many of us crowded around the kitchen table and one by one they each began to sing. Sweet, heart-filled voices soared to fill the room. These poignant and haunting melodies were a precious communication of the soul. No need to understand the words, only a meeting of heart-to-heart there in the moment, uniting sisters of the Earth. A deep knowing which required no intellectual understanding, no political cause, but rather just sisters in the oneness of the moment; a mutual joining without judgment or rivalry.

After several hours of travel by bus we arrived in Okunyova in the early hours of the morning. The group was to gather at an erected temple that was close by. The site consisted of a tall bell tower with a fire pit built into the earth beneath it. We gathered around the fire and to honor the place Carol did a water ceremony, merging waters from the local river Tara with waters from Canada and the Chalice Well in Glastonbury. The Tara River, so aptly named, seemed to exude a mystical energy. Its smooth flowing current seemed to share a heightened energy with the weary pilgrims. After the ceremony the group would return to Omsk, but the Canadians would stay on at Rasma's Ashram which was devoted to Babe Ji.

Rasma had been called by Baba Ji to come from her home in Latvia to set up an ashram in this remote village in Russia; I was at once struck by her courage. She said the area was very special, that she had experienced many mysterious things, including unusual light phenomena when visited by powerful guardians. She was later told by her teachers they were called The Four Directions of Knowledge. When Rasma had first come to this area she had stayed out in a tent. It was here that she experienced this event. Her teachers also told her of intriguing mysteries connected to the nearby lake, where local legend tells of an ancient city lying buried beneath the lake's deep waters. This special area is said to be connected to the Monkey God, Hanuman – some even thinking it could be the birthplace of this powerful God. One day Rasma found a large stone bust shaped in the form of Hanuman.

Soon we prepared for evening prayers, attended by several old grandmothers and children. I was again able to witness a natural synthesis of faiths as the old women recited their rosaries amidst the Eastern teachings. Next morning it was decided we would go back to the temple. Upon arrival we formed a circle around the fire pit, giving thanks for the joining of circles; the joining of East and of West. As I moved around the circle calling out the Four Directions with the drum, the energy of the river and the land seemed to come in to cradle us. Suddenly we were moved into a place of ancient rhythm, seemingly taken completely out of the present place and time. We sensed the ancient pulse of the land, like a primordial dance of energy, and it was weaving a magical circle around our small circle. In that special moment we had been taken back to the memory of the ancestors, dancing with the ancestors, fully immersed in their ancient magic there in this sacred place. A full connection to old traditions and the land.

All too soon it was time to leave. After sad farewells, anticipating too the farewells in Omsk, I realized how hard it was to leave the beauty of such a special place. Amidst these thoughts I was again reminded of the paradox that was Russia. Hardship, poverty, and mysticism standing side by side, creating this rich mix of life in Russia – creating the experience that shaped the Russian soul. On this first segment of my journey these heart-centered people had taught me much about giving and receiving, about lessons of rich community. More important still, I had been given a new awareness about the subtle world. In many places the veil between the worlds was thin and it was helping me now to see in a whole new way!

After a full six weeks I was finally back in Canada. On my first morning home I was awakened by a song from the Throat Singer coming to me on the airwaves. How did he know the exact day I would be back in Canada? How indeed! I recalled the beautiful words of Nicholas Roerich while listening to the Throat Singer's song. *"We will remember you at sunrise; you remember us at sunset."* (3)

Let journey continue! Ho!

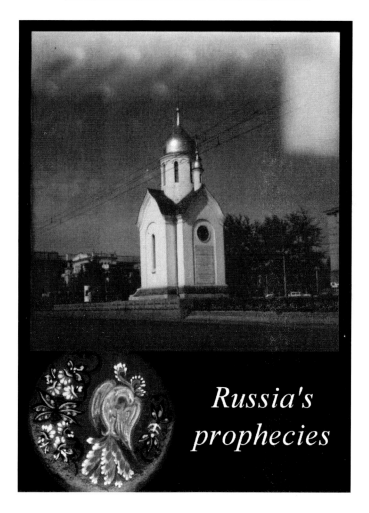

The dream is unending, yet so simple
East joining West. M.W.

The Lesson:

A curious phenomenon happens after the initial steps of the journey – it all disappears. There is then a period of time when the journey becomes illusive – visions and thoughts of the journey seem to vanish. It becomes a period of gestation, much like the actual awaiting of birth. It is a time of integrating, filling, and waiting.

The journey had indeed come to a grinding halt. In fact, it had simply vanished. Eventually, after this difficult period, I got word of an international conference called the Healing Summit, to be held in Glastonbury. It was a wonderful reunion with friends from Russia. I decided to attend a workshop to be given by my friend Galina from Siberia. As lights dimmed, pictures of the Altai began to unfold before me, pictures of incredible beauty, complete with a panorama of wildflowers within the craggy formations of old rolling hills. Emotion welled up inside me for I knew I was being called once more to the journey.

After the conference I joined a friend to travel to the Scilly Isles. This was a group of islands strung together like a necklace, located off the tip of Cornwall. They were considered special in that they were the last stronghold of Goddess worship long after it had been replaced elsewhere by Christianity. We crossed by boat at the tail end of a hurricane, so the crossing was incredibly rough. Once settled at St Mary's I was still feeling woozy, so I lay down for a short rest. I fell into a deep sleep, almost immediately going into the place of dream. I found myself back in a very ancient time – one which predated the Celtic ruins there on the island by thousands of years. I was in what appeared to be a very modern city. Huge pillars of marble, all exquisitely carved, lined the entrance to this beautiful, majestic metropolis. Huge marble pillars full of color and incredible works of art festooned the avenues. Disaster, however, seemed to have struck this ancient place. The very earth trembled and shook, shaking all structures to their very core. The landscape became one of horror as these magnificent buildings began to topple as others started to burn. Dense heavy smoke and scenes of devastation filled the streets. As pieces of the huge pillars began to rain down on the people they were screaming and running in mindless panic trying to get away. Pandemonium reigned.

Within this catastrophe, my dream focused on a single young woman who was also frightened and running. Her name was Mauri. Something was pushing her to get to the temple in time. She quickly ran out of the city limits and up to the place of the Holy of the Holies. Although in a state of panic, she knew that she must reach the Sacred Flame.

Finally reaching the temple entrance she bowed down in reverence to her dear Mother, immediately feeling warmth and protection surrounding her. Then she arose, entering the temple and quickly moved along, past the place of worship, into the inner sanctum. This was the most sacred place in the temple. It was here that the cauldron resided; the cauldron with its Eternal Flame burning there for always, a constant reminder of connection. Mauri knelt down in front of the cauldron. It was quiet, despite the destruction that waged its mighty onslaught outside. She felt a moment of fear and tried to calm herself. How could she, a mere apprentice, dare to come to this place – the Holy of Holies? Why had spirit insisted that she come?

In the quiet and peace of this holy place, with her head bowed humbly, she asked for guidance. She heard the quiet yet distinct voice of the Ancients, "Mauri, your time here on Earth is now finished. The time of your people is finished, but the memory of the flame must live on. You must take an ember from the sacred cauldron. Take it as if it was a spark of fire, a spark to be merged with your DNA. The memory of the Ancient Ones and the connection to the flame will be lost over eons, hidden until it is time. Know little one, you must carry the memory of the Sacred Flame to share this memory with other sisters."

Mauri reached into the beautiful cauldron and picked up the precious ember, totally oblivious of any heat or pain. She felt only the merger of the flame with her body, merging deep within the DNA of the sisterhood, to be held over lifetimes, clear and strong, until the day would once again come as a call from the Great Mother of Us All, to once again bring the flame alive.

"Dear Mauri, you are the keeper of the Sacred Flame. You will keep this over lifetimes, held dear in your heart, cradling the ember of hope within the chalice of your breast, passed on from sister to sister, lineage of hope, lineage of spirit; hidden until the time of a great new era. We love you. Know we will be with you always."

Within the silence of this sacred temple Mauri felt peace at last. Yes, the tradition of the Sacred Flame would live on. It would continue despite the hardship and trials of lifetimes. It was destined to return again…

I awoke from this powerful dream drenched in sweat with my whole body shaking uncontrollably. The dream was deep, reaching back to the Ancients. Did part of the journey encompass hope for a new time – a new paradigm? Perhaps we all possessed that spark, remnants from the Sacred Flame.

In the not so distant past people who claimed that spark, who claimed connection to spirit, were horribly persecuted, or worse – arrested and burned. With threat of such grave consequences etched into our psyche, it was not surprising it became easier to forget. Suddenly the journey was taking on a deeper meaning, providing a greater understanding of fire. We could all dream of once again igniting the flame – creating a new paradigm which encouraged our aliveness and passion. Could we truly step into a new story?

I was beginning to understand the complexities of this new journey. I recalled sometime earlier my friend Galina had come for a brief visit to North America. While here, she had come to my small island for a short stay. During her visit we discussed the prophecies of Edgar

Cayce. I remembered reading a book called *Edgar Cayce's Story of the Origin and Destiny of Man*. It was about the predictions of this new time.

In 1944 he predicted: *"In Russia there comes the hope of the world, not as that sometimes termed the Communistic, or the Bolshevistic, no, but freedom, freedom in that each man will live for his fellow man! The principle has been born. It will take years for it to be crystallized, but out of Russia comes again the hope of the world..."* (Edgar Cayce Reading #3976-29.) (1)

This same prophecy was again reiterated in the book, *Edgar Cayce Predicts – Your Role in Creating the New Age* by Mark Thurston. *"On Russia's religious development will come the greater hope of the world. The one or group that is closer in its relationships may fare better in the gradual changes and final settlement of conditions as the rule of the world."* (Edgar Cayce Reading #3976-10.) (2)

Travelling again to Russia I needed to see first-hand what encompassed the "hope of the world." According to Eastern teachings every country has its own predestined plan and Russia is referred to in many of the ancient teachings as the New Country. What were the treasures held in this vast land which would bring forth such an amazing destiny? How did this impact on my own journey into fire?

As I had written of earlier, in Shamanic tradition you are initially taken back – back to the days of the Ancient Ones, freeing the knots blocking the path so you can then move forward. My dream had done just that, reminding me that there was so much more than the ordinary. I merely had to be open to remembering, and then humbly retrace the footsteps of the ancestors.

Let the journey continue! Ho!

Chapter 7 – A Journey within the Journey

Above: Lake Teletskoe, in the Altai

Left: Montana and our guide Serge

Golden Lake of deep mystery, in the pearl of the dream
Eclipse of the soul, conjunction rings true. M.W.

aching an initiation of the journey's teachings, one goes complex preparation and healing. The foundation of the Shamanic journey lies in the basic teachings of the medicine wheel – the teachings of balance. The medicine wheel is divided into quadrants called the Four Directions. The East and West are designated male and female, and the North and South symbolize spirit and matter. Within the context of "as above, so below" and "as inside, so outside," the student strives to attain balance within the Four Directions, becoming the whole self in the middle.

"Looking back to all that has occurred to me since that eventful day, I am scarcely able to believe in the reality of my adventures. They were truly so wonderful that even now I am bewildered when I think of them." (1)

This quote describes what I came to call my journey within the journey. My return to Russia, although coming in the form of a mini Healing Summit to be held in Novosibirsk, also provided this unusual adventure. It was giving me an experience needed to complete the lesson of balance between the inner male and female. My friend Carol and I would arrive in Siberia a week before the Summit. We would travel with Galina into the Altai, hoping to be in that area for the eclipse of the sun. Many people all over the world looked forward to this special event. In the UK friends there were creating a special celebration before travelling on to Siberia for the Healing Summit.

The Altai Republic, a state in the Russian Federation, has a population of approximately two hundred thousand people. Situated in the Southwest of Siberia, bordering China, Mongolia, and Kazakhstan, this sparsely populated region with its exquisite virgin land is called by its indigenous people "the navel of the world." We were travelling overnight by train to Baurnel and then by bus, which would take us on a six hour journey to a small village called Artybash – our destination.

This village was situated at the headwaters of Biya, the only river that flows out of Lake Teletskoe. Exhausted, we finally arrived in the tiny village of Artybash, but it was too late to get to our cabin by the lake so the village Healer and her daughter told Galina we could stay with them. It was a large house close to the water and surrounded by an immense garden. They were a family of Old Believers. They welcomed us into their home, decorated in the lovely tradition of painted ceilings, the old Russian designs bright with vivid colors.

Next morning, while waiting for the boat to take us to our base camp the women explained that Zhanna, the daughter, along with her father, would travel each fall up the Chulyshman River at the other end of the lake. There they would collect precious herbs needed for healing remedies and teas. Her mother was a gifted Healer serving a large community. She had studied the Tibetan healing arts extensively.

The boat arrived the following morning and we made our way up the coastline of Lake Teletskoe. How beautiful it was – rugged, yet delicate, captured in the silence of pristine wilderness. On arrival at our destination we quickly arranged to meet a local boatman who would take us on a tour of the rest of the lake.

The boatman arrived after lunch. He had dark hair, a muscular build and was dressed in a striped cotton shirt which made him look more like a gypsy than a local guide. He was respectful, yet somehow appeared mischievous, which gave the impression that he was really laughing at the world. Although insistent that he was a Christian I got the impression that underneath there was someone knowledgeable in the ways of Shamanic tradition. It was arranged that we would start early the next morning.

Prior to beginning our new adventure I had prepared a small black pouch with some sage to present to Sergei, our guide. This was customary in Shamanic tradition when wishing to honor the person's wisdom and knowledge. He acknowledged the gift with a curt nod.

So started our journey on the lake called the Pearl; a journey which slowly took on a mystical quality which seemed to override the discomforts of a bumpy boat ride. Our first stop was a small research station where we met the director whose name was Vladimir. They had all been there for some time, but like others, had lost their funding with the economic collapse. They managed to continue through the generosity of friends, but it meant the village had electricity only while using the computers. They described the area as being very special, speaking of unusual light phenomena. We were told that it was not unusual to see huge pillars of light in the night sky.

Next we arrived at a small finger of land jutting out into the lake. On one side of it a mountain with no name overlooked a rushing turbulent river of sparkling blue and white water. The river was called Kokshy. It was at Kokshy, where we stopped for gas, that we met Montana. Montana was a big blue eyed giant. Towering over our guide Sergei – who himself was over six feet – he came down to the waters edge to greet us and invite us for tea.

This gentle giant had lived in the area as a hermit for five years. He had been born in the area of Ob Lake, outside Novosibirsk, one of seven children. He had tired of city life and had moved to this remote spot. He felt the Kokshy River was like Belevodye – the mystical running white waters often spoken of in Russia. Like the scientists, he too had often seen beams of energy coming from across the lake. Montana was of Indian Slavic ancestry. He was very interested in North American Indian tradition and called himself a "warrior of the heart."

During our conversation he spoke of the Babas, the stone carvings that we had seen at the Museum Under the Stars, telling us that they had been taken from a place nearby. He invited us to stay, but we had to continue.

Our next stops would be Big and Little Chile, meaning glass or mirror. Quickly we made our way across to the other side of the lake. While Carol puttered close to the shore, Galina and I made our way in through the forest. Again the water was rushing from a river similar to the Kokshy, its melody pervading the area with its sound. Inside a small grove of birch trees were several old stones, lying in what seemed to have once been an old stone circle. Galina called me over to look at one of the stones. It appeared to be rather special. Etched on top of it was the distinct form of a cross. I put my hand on top of the stone and was instantly amazed by the energy that poured into the palm of my hand. It was a gurgling, rippling action, quite palpable.

Next we were drawn to the edge of the small stand of trees. We had come face to face with a high, dense wall. The wall, although somewhat porous, was totally devoid of any vegetation and appeared man-made. It was strange seeing this solid concrete wall out in the wilderness. Both Galina and I walked along the edge of the wall, drawn towards something, though we weren't sure what. Was it a gateway? Were we being guided to an opening? When we spoke of this experience later we both realized we had been pulled in search of an opening. We both sensed that an opening would have taken us up, up into the chimney and into the interior of the mountain. Suddenly we heard Sergei calling us, saying it was time to go.

Quickly taking some pictures of the place, we left, both of us still uncertain of what it was we had stumbled onto.

In talking to Sergei about our experience he then told us he had lived in the area of big Chile for several months. One day he had what he called a hallucination. It appeared to be more than that. Each time he thought of a certain song it would magically appear in his head in full orchestra rendition. This unusual music, so like the music of the spheres, continued for a full day. The veil here seemed thin indeed!

Soon we pulled into shore again, to a camp, this time to be greeted by a small family group. They invited us to tea. While waiting, I decided to take a walk along the edge of the lake. I turned the corner and was suddenly confronted by two angry, large black dogs. They bounded towards me, barking and snarling with teeth bared. Despite being terrified, I stood my ground, and in a loud voice told them to stop. On the third try of saying, "No, stop it!" they somehow ceased the aggressive behavior and simply ran off in a different direction. I stood motionless and silent for a minute, feeling totally shaken. With this extremely unwelcome greeting, I explored no further. Back near the water's edge we had tea, curiously served from a fine bone china teapot; we were, however, happy to be on our way.

We were now making our way towards the end of the lake. Lake Teletskoe is not wide, but it is very long. We were edging our way down the lake, meandering alongside the banks in a winding path which took us up through an incredible vista of mountains on either side. As we continued, there were spectacular waterfalls in several places, where water fell in a great rush down to the lake. We were going up the Chulyshman River of which Zhanna had spoken, where she and her father collected their healing herbs. Our destination was a place called Arzhan spring. Here the mud was said to have healing qualities, especially for irritations of the skin. In the past it had been a resort where people would come for rest, and for the healing properties of this special mud.

As we rounded a corner many, many prayer ties came into view, fluttering on the low lying branches. We pulled over and got out. It was like moving into the past. Tubs lay empty, now unused, where once they were used for mud treatments. Now, without the funding, this special work could not continue, so the area again lay fallow. I spent some time at openings, where water trickled out of the earth. I put out prayers, offering my own prayer ties in honor of this beautiful spring and her healing qualities. Sergei went to gather wild herbs and flowers for both Carol and I, telling us we needed these plants to heal. This Christian Shaman displayed a great wealth of knowledge about herbal medicine. We gathered water, mud, and herbs and then moved into the boat to make our way back.

Our final destination was a place called Bele, meaning family. It was here that Sergei had promised we would see some Babas. Rounding a slight curve of the lake, high up on the cliffs we saw strange Baba-like stones, forming a distinct outline on the horizon. Soon a small dock came into view as we reached Bele, our final destination.

Clambering out of the small boat we followed a steep path, moving up to a village. Wildflowers in many shades scattered the path as we made our way upward. Soon Carol found it too steep a climb, so turned back. I too found it steep, but thoughts of seeing the Babas, however, gave me incentive to continue.

Once at the top, Galina and I were greeted by a young couple. He was a Shaman and together with his wife Natasha, they called themselves the Keepers of Nature. They lived here on top of the world amidst a large apple orchard. It seemed incredible to me that apples could grow at such a high altitude. Natasha took us down a road past the apple trees to show us the Babas. The view from this mountaintop village was almost ethereal. It was as I had imagined seeing the Himalayas for the first time and I was in total awe. High peaks casting shades of purple, beige, and pink that seemed to bless this land of the Altai with pure spirit. Across from the orchard, sitting off by themselves, were two small Baba stones. Natasha told us that just this past spring the female stone had developed a small crack along her face. She said it was like this ancient stone was crying for humanity, and indeed this is what it looked like. The image was like a gentle tear that was running down her craggy face.

As we thanked Natasha, the clouds were suddenly heavy and menacing. It had become dark, the sky overcast, as if a summer thunderstorm was coming. Natasha quickly guided us into her home to take refuge. We arrived just in time as the rain began streaming down in torrents.

Time passed and eventually the rain began to ease. It was then we saw Sergei walking quickly along the path. He was out of breath and seemed extremely angry, shouting at us, asking why we had taken so long. He was most concerned about Carol, who had been left stranded back at the boat. We quickly made our farewells and headed back down to the boat, only to find Carol drenched from the downpour. Things were extremely tense. In total silence we clambered into the boat and headed out once more. After profuse apology, extended from both of us, Carol seemed to take it all in her stride, but Sergei remained silent, worried about the lateness of the day and the advancing darkness. Finally he suggested we would have to go back to Montana's where we would spend the night.

Soon dusk descended and we approached Montana's cabin in total darkness. Sergei called out, and Montana, who had been asleep, came out to see who had arrived. Seemingly taking the arrival of three women and a boatman in his stride, we were invited in and soon he had a fire going, tea on the boil and beds made up for all of us. Crisp, white sheets magically appeared out of nowhere. Soon the men left to sleep at a nearby cabin and then, warmed by tea, we were off to sleep.

We would spend a full day on this little jut of land, close to the mountain with no name and the beautiful white water of the Kockshy. Immersed in nature, it became a special time for prayer, meditation, and soulful solitude while these two brusque men totally cared for us, even treating us to freshly caught fish from the lake.

Sadly, it was time to return to base camp, so again we made our farewells, leaving Montana and this special land of spirit.

Suddenly it dawned on us that we were approaching the time for the eclipse of the sun. It seems that I along with my sisters – one from the UK, and one from Russia – along with our boatman, would experience this event out in the middle of the lake. There, nestled on the waters of the Pearl, we would get to witness this unique sacred marriage of nature.

The eclipse of the sun – the bringing together of the sun and the moon in visible conjunction – has since ancient times represented the sacred marriage. Both Annie Besant and Margaret Starbird make reference to this unique conjunction (2). In this brief display in the cosmos, we were to witness the powerful joining of the masculine and feminine energies. In the middle of the lake, like the pilgrims we were, we sat and watched with complete awe as the skies brought in this incredible union of the dark and light – perfect blend of male and female, perfect marriage for above and below. Carol had brought some special water from Glastonbury's Chalice Well and she proceeded to pour the water into the lake, creating for us our own special joining there in nature. Huge dark clouds boiled up and instantly formed a deep tunnel, as a circle of light became surrounded, etched in the middle of the dark clouds. Nature bringing us the purity of light shining through the darkness. We watched in silence, each in our own way. The journey within the journey had culminated in this sacred marriage of sun and moon, male and female. Margaret Starbird describes the ancient world as depicting divinity as the union of opposites (3). In that divine moment when male marries female there is a magical instant when spirit reaches down and blesses the Earth. Lessons of the union of male and female in this mystical and ancient land. As the journey continued to move ever forward, glimmerings of a new understanding began to appear. An understanding of why this amazing land was being dubbed the New Country.

My beautiful land of Russia, I am honored and I am full. May the journey continue. Ho!

Chapter 8 – The Mother of the World

Mt. Belukha, holy mountain

My revered bow is full of love, for those above and those below.
The ladder built on sacred trust, to reach the gates of those most
high. M.W.

The Lesson:

Now turning to the other two quadrants of the medicine wheel, to
focus on balancing spirit and matter. One doesn't merely reach up,

rather one invites spirit to come down and join us on Earth. It is then that the student, through prayer and ceremony, can begin to move into collaboration with spirit, ultimately achieving balance.

In continuing the lessons of balance, another adventure would surface – this time going to the top of Mount Belukha. Towards the end of the conference we would again travel into the Altai, stopping at Lake Aya. Lake Aya is a tiny lake shrouded on all sides with rock and trees. Its surface is like a mirror, hiding the depth of its mystery. Locals say that Aya, along with Lake Baikal, are the only lakes on the planet that have tectonic plates at the very bottom of them. Perhaps due to these plates, there is a mysterious spiral-like current ever present in the lake. Stories abound about many people who have disappeared in the lake, never to be found. Like Lake Baikal, Aya is surrounded by mystery.

During our stay at Aya, Roy Little Sun – a delegate of the conference – wished to hold a special ceremony on the swinging bridge that spanned the Katun River which flowed near Lake Aya. This man, a Shaman originally from Indonesia but who now travelled the world promoting peace, had officiated many beautiful ceremonies through the Summit. He now wished to pay tribute to the legend of the river. *"Where the final battle would be fought on the Katun River and we would then have peace."*(1) Plans were also being made to fly to the top of Mount Belukha after our short stay at Aya.

Early the next morning a small group of us went out to the bridge. The men went to the other end and we, the women, stayed at the end closest to the resort – both groups meeting in the center of the bridge. Roy had the stem of his ceremonial pipe and I had the bowl, so when we met in the center we could then join the pipe as a symbolic way of joining the male and the female energies. Roy also felt it would be symbolic of moving from the old era to the new one, an era of the Feminine Principles. With moving from the dominant male patterns to a balancing with the feminine energies this would be achieved, as so many Earth Elders felt needed to happen.

Each of us started the long walk along the bridge to meet in the center. As we came together Roy put out prayers and had a bundle to throw into the Katun, the mighty river of legend and of hope, whose name means "female" in Turkic. We had waited for sunrise, and as the sun peeped out through the middle of the mountains, the bundle went into the turbulent current below. Two pieces of the peace pipe joined in balance.

We were later told that while we were doing ceremony on the bridge, the little white dog (the mascot of the resort) and her pups had all lined up in a row and howled in unison for a full minute in honor of the ceremony – full circle with all sentient beings. It is not for us to understand how these things happen.

With the ceremony complete we were informed all arrangements were complete. We would be flying to the top of Mount Belukha. All over the planet there are places that possess a certain energy which seems to call us. They are known as power spots. I know when I have been blessed with coming upon these places; there is an insistent tugging, which can only be described as a yearning to be there, and quickly. It is as if there was some invisible cord that attaches one to the location, ever calling you. Upon reaching the spot you are never quite the same. Mount Belukha, considered the sacred mountain of Russia, is one such place.

The name Belukha means "white" in Russian. It is considered the spiritual heart of Altai. Sought out by many, it stands as the "Abode of Purity, Beauty, and Light." It is often referred to symbolically as the Divine Mother of the World. There are many legends told of this special mountain. Long, long ago, the Goddess Umai and her husband Altaidyng lived in a place in the Northern part of the Altai. One day Ker-Dyutpa, often depicted as a fish or a monster that held the Earth on its back, started to change the Earth's climate. It began to snow and get very cold, which was most unusual. Before, in the Altai it had always been warm and the trees and the grass were always green. Altaidyng Aazi decided he must go to the Sky, to the Bourkhans (Gods) and ask for help. He climbed higher and higher, going from one Bourkhan to another looking for the Lord Kudai. Meanwhile it was becoming colder and colder in Altai, and Umai, in order to save her children, changed their four daughters and two sons into rocks. She then took her two remaining daughters into her arms and fled to the south of Altai. During the perils of the journey, however, they all froze and were turned into a huge glacier with three summits. The one in the middle is said to be Umai's head, while the two adjoining peaks are those of her daughters. This mountain has since become known as Belukha. In the vicinity of Belokurikha, where the other children were turned to stones, is another rock called Ker-Dyumpa, which resembles a dragon. Since the time of this great tragedy, the loving heart of the Mother Goddess Umai continues to beat in the white holy mountain of Belukha.

Unlike the mountain range so similar to a mother's breast, which loomed above us during our sunrise ceremony on the Katun River, the peaks of Belukha are like the Mother's crown, similar to ancient drawings of the crown of Om Mai and Ishtar. Some legends say that Mount Belukha is the mystical abode of the Altai Sisters, while others say the Altai Sisters come from the Golden Mountain – a mystery which would unfold later.

It was with all of this mystery in mind that I looked forward to travelling to this sacred mountain with much expectant anticipation. We made our way to the airport outside Gorno-Altaisk where a huge, ancient, battered helicopter awaited us. The plan was that we would make two landings on Mount Belukha; one on the Kazakhstan side and one on the Russian slope. It would take much of the day to do this.

Feeling much trepidation, we were soon, however, airborne, flying towards the magnificent mountain range of the Altai Mountains. I watched the vista of the landscape below spread out in the bright morning sun. Patterns of rock were etched out on the face of the Earth, and snaking right through the middle was the beautiful Katun, steadfast and true, marking the way of this blessed journey. It was an incredible sight seeing the reflection of the sacred Altai lands spread out before us, giving us a unique aerial view of the region. As we gained height I began to see bright blue dots, looking like turquoise jewels embedded in the sides of the mountain slopes. These were small clusters of lakes scattered along the unending mountain range.

Climbing higher I began to feel great discomfort breathing. My breath was now coming in short shallow gasps. Was it the altitude? Just as I was about to panic, tears slowly began to slide down my cheeks. All of the struggle and doubts of actually making it to the top of this majestic mountain seemed to wash away, washing away those emotions that held my earthly struggle.

Soon we could see the white tips of the mountain range and the helicopter began circling, preparing to land. Getting out, we looked from the top of the mountain as it sloped away before us. We began walking around, appreciating this magnificent picture of nature, taking in the low lying shrubs and wildflowers that even this high were determined to bloom. I walked towards a small pool of water, spending time connecting to the amazing spirit of this place, but soon we were given a signal that it was time to leave. Time to move to the Russian side of the mountain.

After some time the pilot called to us and Galina explained that we were now approaching the peaks on the Russian side. Taking my turn to move forward, I looked out on the vista below us. Mere words cannot describe the wonder of these mighty peaks. I looked down, speechless, taking in the resplendent nature of Belukha's mighty triple crown. How blessed we were to see her this close. Out of the misty caverns of history came the words of Helena Roerich: *"She beckons to her children from far-distant fields: Hasten, children! I wish to teach you. I have keen eyes and alert ears ready for you. Sit ye down upon My garment. Let us learn to soar!"* (2)

The helicopter had come to a stop beside a large lake, its surface a cloudy, milky white in color, nestled at the foot of the triple peaks of the mountain. Upon landing, I set off down a trail along the edge of the lake. As I walked I took in the panorama surrounding me. I had not gone far when I noticed a large rock out in the water. It seemed alive with energy and appeared to be pointing – but pointing to what? I looked over into what seemed like a small enclosure. This powerful spot seemed to be almost physically pulling me into its center. I climbed up over some rocks strewn in the entrance and before me stood a beautiful waterfall. The water splashed down over the rocks, its rhythm of sound creating an inner stillness for all who ventured there. Very special indeed! Moving over to a patch of land in front of the waterfall, I sat down; I had been drawn here, pulled to

71

this very spot to honor our Mother above, but somehow it seemed very familiar. Suddenly it dawned on me. This little spot on the edge of Lake Accem was identical to the spot I had visited for many years back in Canada, on the tiny island where I lived. They were mirrors of each other!

Enjoying this unique coincidence, I spread out the things I wanted to use for this special ceremony. In creating the sacred circle I put my prayers out to the beautiful Mother of Us All, to Mother Mary and my beloved Mary Magdalene – the triple feminine in honor of the triple crown. I felt such gratitude for the opportunity to connect to this magical doorway of the sacred.

Ceremony complete, I sat quietly in the serene presence of this place. What was the mystery that lay beyond the magic of the waterfall? Could this be a gateway to Shambalha, the place called Kapala or White Island, sacred abode of the Masters? Some believed that going to Shambalha was to go inward to a pure place in your heart. Others believed there were actually two Shambalhas – one of them being very much in the realm of the physical. I do know I had never experienced anything quite so profound. Enveloped in this potent atmosphere, high on the mountaintop, made one aware of a certain vibratory energy that was far beyond anything I had before experienced. It exuded an aliveness, changing perceptions of nature's beauty in a whole new way.

A vision of beauty, a truth in our hearts,
White Island of hope, where the truth really starts. M.W.

I became aware that our time here was moving to a close, so I began walking back from the waterfall. As I went along the trail beside Lake Accem I once again beheld the vista of Mount Belukha. The peak was like a huge throne, with the crown of the triple peaks on top. Pearly white waters were flowing down from the throne to join the milky white waters of Lake Accem. I stood stock still, for suddenly I understood what I was seeing. I was witnessing a natural replication of the Milky Way! As above, so below!

How remarkable to realize that this natural phenomenon existed here in Russia. Here was the mirror of the Milky Way sitting on top of this holy mountain. From the triple crown of the Great Mother of Us All comes the milky white water of Accem, cascading down into Accem Lake. The lake then feeds into the Accem River, which disappears into the mountain to reappear and spring forth in the mighty headwaters of the River Katun. The Katun, in turn, flows across the Altai.

What is the hidden meaning behind these natural mirrors of the Milky Way that are seen in nature? I find it remarkable that our ancestors had mapped out the reflection of the Milky Way in many areas of the planet, creating a natural alchemy of as above, so below. Judith Polich's book, *Return of the Children of the Light*, describes the following: *"When the light below equals the light above, the*

73

gates between the worlds open. " (3) Perhaps our ancestors knew this. I do know I was shown Earth's collaboration with spirit – ultimately, my authentic lessons of balancing the physical with spirit.

May the journey continue. Ho!

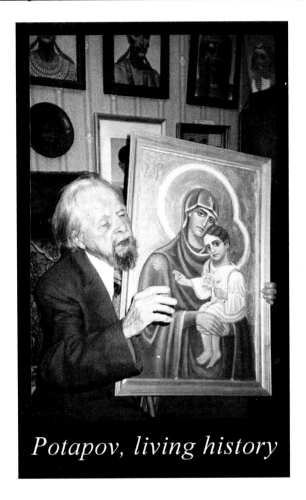

Potapov, living history

Come to the circle, no beginning – no end

Casting the magic, where the dream never ends. M.W.

The Lesson:

Ceremony and celebration are an intrinsic part of the journey. Aided by voice and drum, they add to the potency, the quickening of the journey.

Quickening is a heightened state of awareness in the body. It is the awakening of instinctual powers, reclaiming our intuitive abilities – all of which guides the student forward towards the ultimate initiation. This process that we have been so long cut off from is greatly enhanced by ceremony and celebration. As I moved towards the end of my second trip in Russia, several experiences would highlight this phenomenon.

Several had been invited to present workshops at the conference. I had chosen to conduct a workshop on the Shamanic circle, as experienced within Earth based spirituality. As the room began to fill to overflowing, I called out the Four Directions, picked up feather and smudge bowl, and began to smudge each participant in the circle. As the sacred smoke moved in and around us, joining each of us in the circle, the energy in the room heightened. Sparks of light began to bounce off the mirrors in the room, seeming to announce the arrival of invisible grandmothers and grandfathers. This heightened energy lent itself to a meeting of East and West, joining from the heart. As my dear friend from Omsk would later relate,

"The energy was such that night, it was if we were showered with pure liquid light." An amazing circle of celebration.

The talk I gave that night was quite incidental to the transforming energy of the circle. I spoke of the concepts of totems and oneness; that we, as humans, had forgotten that we were just a very small part of the circle. I described the Tree of Life and how this very ancient symbol helped us to connect spirit with matter, but mostly I focused on the sacredness of the circle. *The Teachings of Agni Yoga* emphasize just how sacred and powerful the circle is (1). All wisdom traditions honor the circle. It is from this ancient wisdom that we can finally begin to experience co-creation with spirit, so clearly witnessed in the circle that night as we came together from a place of heart.

During the Healing Summit I had again met Andrew from Omsk. He was inviting us to his city and his center on our way back to Moscow. Andrew had established the Avicenna Healing Center in Omsk, where we had met on my first trip to Russia. Andrew described his work which he simply called "touching" – a unique approach to healing that embraces body, mind, and spirit. He further described this method as being like a wave or pulse of energy which would help bring the body back into harmony. He likened it to an imitation of the gentle movement one would feel as a baby being rocked and cradled by its mother.

Healing always proved to be very powerful in Russia. Due perhaps because the healing became enhanced by the complete openness of the people, coupled with the very special land in many areas. I recall doing a healing on an old grandmother in the village of Kaurai. She explained that since the time of her surgery, some months before, she had not felt well. She then proceeded to lift up her top to show me her surgical scar. Words fail to describe my horror and shock. Her skin was raised in huge angry welts where the incision had been made. This, coupled with dead white scar tissue, made it look as if someone had tried to carve some macabre map on her ample belly. It would take several years to learn the mystery behind this barbarous scarring. It had nothing to do with the skills of the surgeons; rather, it had everything to do with the lack of proper supplies for stitching the incision. Abject poverty was what marked her. Sadly, I would see several of these horrific scars.

I remember placing my hands on the lady's stomach where she had described experiencing the discomfort. The very instant I made contact low gut wrenching sobs welled up in my body. I just sobbed and sobbed. With the crying, an even stranger thing began to happen. As I cried, the grandmother's face began to transform. The tension in her face began to leave and suddenly she transformed into someone that appeared to be at least ten years younger than she had been prior to the healing touch. This dear grandmother simply smiled and said she felt much better. "Spacibo!" (Thank you!)

Later, describing this exchange of energy and the subsequent healing to Carol, we both concluded it was the grandmothers here who seemed to hold the pain for both the land and the Russian people. They had certainly kept the spark of spirituality alive during the years of Communism. They were the keepers of the sacred during this time, when they passed on hymns, prayers, and psalms, as well as ancient folk wisdom. They kept the deep reverence and love of Russia's rich spiritual traditions alive.

Now, having arrived at the Avicenna Healing Center, Andrew wished to demonstrate healing through sound. He suggested that a group of women Healers join me in a circle. He proceeded to link us up somehow energetically. As energy became heightened around the circle he invited me to sing a song. The sound emanating from my body was crystal clear. It was truly profound. What was making the circle and my voice so potent?

The energy we all felt was indeed transformational. Despite our language barrier I was able to understand that each of us in the circle had something in common. We each had a connection to Mary. For me it was to Mary Magdalene, for others it was to the Mother Mary, but by connecting us energetically we had somehow tapped into this higher source connection. This simple connection which helped to create such a healing sound brought with it a power, a simple beauty, and a container of mystical energy. This had likely always been known by the ancient Healers of our distant past, but was again here to remind us that it was possible to tap into a higher energy source for healing.

In healing I believe we must move to the place of heart – to what the Agni Yoga teachings call the chalice. When we call in our guidance, calling to an energy of a pure and higher source, we are calling from a place of love and of reverence. We then tap into a pure source of wisdom for healing. By moving into the subtle levels the Healer becomes the conduit which opens the channels to an experience of alchemy. Thus, with renewed balance and the raising of vibratory energy, healing begins.

Soon it was time to make fond farewells and travel to the final stop on our journey, a place called Perm; a city in the heart of the Urals. Perm, like Omsk, had been a closed city; foreigners had not been allowed into these cities until quite recently. Perm is also significant geographically. It is the natural division between Europe and Asia given that the rivers change their flow of direction here. Perm then acts like the doorway to Siberia.

Exhausted by the many miles of travel, once settled at our home-stay we soon got ready for bed. Morning arrived and upon my awakening Ilana, our host, arrived with a singing birthday card and flowers. The word had spread that it was my birthday. In Russia they make a big fuss about what they call a jubilee celebration. We were also treated to a special breakfast of birthday cake and gifts.

But celebrations were not to end there. It seems a special outing had been planned. We were to drive a small distance out into the country to a place they called the point of connection. We sped out of the city heading north. After crossing the large River Karma, we veered off onto what appeared to be no road at all – more like a path. There were certainly more potholes than road and we bumped along seemingly unsure of our course or direction. Soon we began to run out of road and quickly began to climb. At last we came out into a clearing, parked and then continued on by foot.

We had arrived at a place with great energy. There was a huge bowl-shaped indentation in the earth. I was told that in ancient times the area had been struck by a meteor. This special place was called the point of connection because it was the convergence point of two rivers, the main one called the River Karma, the other Chusovaya. Tradition suggests that if a person stands on this point of connection, overlooking the great River Karma, they are able to clear their karma.

The view of the rivers was magnificent. Majestic waters flowed together from the two mighty rivers to become one. A physical image of East meeting West. I put out my prayer of gratitude for this incredible journey – also a prayer that perhaps someday soon I would return. Just below the peak our small group stood together in a circle, each expressing our gratitude and appreciation for coming together. I was not to know at that time how we were weaving our future history together.

Once back at the city our celebration continued with an evening gathering with devotees of Sri Baba. We arrived to find a packed room with everyone anxious to meet the foreign women. A large tumbler of water was passed around the circle for each person to offer warm wishes in celebration of the jubilee. I was invited to drink it down in chug-a-lug fashion so I could take in all of those amazing warm wishes from these delightful friends. As the evening closed, a young woman sang a song of praise to Sri Baba called "Mamma Sri." Again I was to experience the delight of crystal sound as her beautiful voice rose up to reach spirit and was able to touch each and every heart in the room.

Next day an expedition had been planned to travel to the north of Perm. On the first leg of the journey we would make a stop to see a famous local artist living in Solikamsk. The artist was Mikhail Potapov and he was ninety-five years old. Both artist and historian, he had lived through much of the history of Russia. He had been put in the prison camps, being first arrested for supposedly disseminating literature on mysticism. He had merely studied theosophy for several years. This gentle, diminutive man was later convicted of counter revolutionary activities and imprisoned for five years. Despite his grave suffering he remains a staunch Tsarist.

Despite his age, the passion he held for his art still burned brightly in his eyes. He had only recently given up trying to paint, as his eyes were failing him. He was called "a traveller between the worlds," and that indeed is what he was. He could recall with great detail attending one of the Tsar's grand balls, remembering the exquisite lighting and the incredibly beautiful dresses the women wore. He stated quite passionately that he felt Communism had destroyed that which was beautiful in his beloved Russia. In his earlier years, he worked restoring many church Icons, but his other passion came from what he felt was a past life in Egypt. Never having seen Egypt, he relied on his inner memories for his amazing Egyptian art.

He took great delight in meeting the two foreign grandmothers and without warning stood up and sang "Rose Marie I Love You." There was, of course, a great twinkle in his eye while he sang. With great reluctance we took our leave, saying goodbye to living history. Both the art and the man had left an indelible impression upon us.

In the morning we travelled further north to a small village, where at the museum we saw exhibits of local Chudd art. As well, there were several ancient Icons – part animal, part saint. In the corner of a small window was an antique rosary, much like the one I had been given. The gift I had been given was rare indeed!

On our way back to Perm, stopping for a picnic en route, Carol asked if I would cast a circle. This was the last circle on the journey. As I walked out the circle, there in the middle of the forest a small white dog strangely appeared, seemingly heralding the completion of a wondrous journey. We had cast our circle from Siberia and back – community, connection, ceremony, and authentic heartfelt celebration!

Now, again we were coming full circle back to Moscow, where we would stay briefly with a young woman we had met at the conference. Her flat was within walking distance of the Roerich museum. We found the museum closed, but like all the other magical occurrences on the journey, arrangements were made for a private showing. We were also invited to have tea with Ludmila Shaposhnikova, writer and director of the museum.

To say I was thrilled would be an understatement. In her late seventies, Ludmila had the energy and passion of a twenty year old. She gave us a brief historic account of the building of the museum and told us that she had taken the same route as the Roerichs through the Altai-Himalayas. She had performed this feat by herself, in her fifties, and it had taken her four years. She had compared places en route with the paintings of Nicholas Roerich. Her dedication to the work of the Roerichs and the teachings of Agni Yoga touched me deeply. Her staff treated this amazing woman with great love and care.

While drinking our tea I told her I had been to the top of Mount Belukha as well as to the mystical area beside Lake Teletskoe. She confirmed both sacred gateways I had witnessed. In making our leave we were presented with many gifts, but they came also with a reminder not to forget Zveringord, the mystical City of Bells. My journey was introducing a new mystery!

In one of the books we had been given there was reference to three circles of blue, a symbol of the secret land of Shambalha. *"The mysterious three circles, the symbol of the secret land, shone with a blue light."*(2) Imagine my surprise when I later discovered a photo of the strange wall at Lake Teletskoe, displaying three prominent blue circles.

Later, once more back at home, I learned sadly from Galina that our reluctant Teletskoe guide, Sergei, had died. He had gone out onto the lake but hadn't returned. All they found was his empty boat. Later Galina tried to retrace our steps around Lake Teletskoe, but couldn't. It had all changed. In remembering Ludmila's affirmation of the portal on Mount Belukha, remembering Chile and what we had experienced there, and fondly recalling my reluctant Shaman with the twinkling eyes, I felt such gratitude for this sacred journey imbued with unique experiences of ceremonies and celebration. Ludmila's urgings rang out in my ears. Remember Zveringod! Remember the City of the Bells!

The onward mystery of the journey would continue. Ho!

On the Silk Road

Awaken my heart, dear Masters of old

The heart is my chalice; of this I've been told. M.W.

The Lesson:

As the lessons of preparation fully impact on the student within her

journey, there is suddenly a huge push forward. This push is called

the shift. Outwardly nothing has changed; inwardly the physical

process, the arousal of inner fire begins.

Back home once again I reviewed the experiences of the past summer, remembering the balance of the inner male and female, recalling the pilgrimage to the top of Mount Belukha, and the balancing of spirit and matter always grounded within the context of ceremony and celebration. It seemed now I craved silence and stillness – something this remote island provided. During this period of gestation there seemed to be a sloughing off, much like the snake shedding its skin. I was ridding myself of old blocks and baggage, becoming free of the old story, of things that just didn't seem to be working anymore.

Lynn Andrews, in her teaching, explained that unlike the raising of the kundalini, which moves up two paths through the body centers, arousal of the inner fire is "experienced as a quickening of the blood."(1) Fire is a form of alchemy, that mysterious change that takes something in one form and transforms it into another (2). In Shamanic traditions this experience is visceral.

My whole body was heating up, much like menopause, but much more intense and relentless. With the heating up came a different kind of clarity. I was seeing color in a whole new way and there was a stronger sense of who I was. It was as if my whole vibratory energy was in some way changing. Learning Shamanically is always experiential. It now became a heating up to work with fire. On the basic physical level this fiery experience – the searing, unyielding heat – continued along with horrific body spasms. Each night, as I lay down to sleep, waves of heat and spasms continuously washed over me. It felt as though every cell in my body was literally being shaken and reshaped as centers in my body awakened. All Shamanic tradition works with one's feminine nature, the place of the intuitive and wisdom. Although it went much deeper, down into the cellular structure, it felt like I was holding a huge ball of fire within my very womb. I was literally being thrown into the fires of the Dark Goddess herself. It was a very difficult process and went on for weeks.

Part of my Shamanic journey has always evolved symbolically through the presence of certain animals. During these challenging times heron became my constant companion. It is said that the heron mirrors the phoenix, the bird of fire which symbolizes the rising out of ashes, the journey of regeneration. One evening during this time of waiting I happened to see two herons perched on the top of the highest trees. They stood like sentinels guarding the doorway to the East.

It was during this time that I had another Shamanic dream. I came to call it the Church of Light. The dream was taking me on a journey to a sacred mountain. Initially, I didn't know I would be taken to a mountain, or where the mountain was situated. In this remarkable dream I found myself on a small boat. I was moving along on a body of water and realized I was being taken around a huge rock formation. Getting out of the boat, I began to walk towards some old ruins – ancient ruins which seemed to be built into the side of a mountain. This old structure appeared to have been a temple or church. A mirror image presented itself, but with a difference; above were the ruins from ancient times, but deep in the side of the mountain was a temple that was intact. This crypt-like formation formed an identical church to the one above, only this space was fully functional and alive. It was also not of this world.

There were windows engraved into the side of the mountain. These beautifully carved windows were made from amazing multicolored crystals. These mysterious crystals seemed to shine, both from within and without, and were able to cast light inside the church. The colors of the crystals were composed of bright, deep hues of greens, blues, and purple. I had never experienced the depth of color these light-filled crystals captured within them. They also held a strange, otherworldly brightness I had never before witnessed.

A small room off the main body of the church contained a fireplace where a fire burnt brightly. It felt quite warm and cozy despite the sense that it was not of the mundane world. As I looked around this small room I noticed some scarves casually draped across an armchair. I went over to examine them more closely. The first one I picked up to look at was a beautiful muted green. It displayed many strange and unknown symbols that had been embroidered on the scarf with jet-black beads. I looked again at the scarves in front of me. This time I chose a larger scarf. As I picked up this burnt amber scarf in its earthy red tones, I held it out in front of me to get a better look. It had on it a large figure of a woman, beside whom was a male figure dressed like a toreador, and a bull – both figures smaller in size than the woman. Just as I was trying to make sense of the pattern on the scarf, a man magically appeared.

I seemed somehow to know this man. He spoke to me, saying that there were only two families now – but to come, we must hurry for it was time for the service. I followed him into the main body of the church where, standing in the very front of the nave, a priest stood. Several people were seated on the church benches, which were tiered, getting lower as they reached down to the front. Here they were at the same level as the priest who was standing before the audience. As he raised his hands he became surrounded with a yellow light which intensified, surrounding the priest-like figure who now became totally engulfed and then disappeared into the light. Now my attention was riveted to one side of the church. There, enclosed in a cubicle was a Christ-like figure slowly being suffused with light. The Christ-like figure glowed intensely. Just as I was becoming totally mesmerized by the light and figure, the man I had originally met began running down to the front of the church. He, along with several members of the audience, had run to the front of the church, just off to the left side. They were assisting the priest in coming back into his physical body as he seemed to be having trouble reappearing in physical form. At last the priest reappeared, and as he did, I woke up.

Shamanic dreams are different from our ordinary dreaming in that they are more vivid and detailed. On these occasions the dreamer is usually given total recall and I believe these special dreams transport us out of time, showing us a place, person, or lesson that is needed at that specific moment in our journey. In my heart I hoped I had been taken into the realms of Shambalha, but I don't know. What I do know, however, is that the Masters were calling this new time the time of fire. Agni Yoga, called the yoga of fire, teaches that we can all link to the fiery virtues of divinity, that we all possess this ability. Our task then, over lifetimes, is to bring this spark alive. Just perhaps this unique and challenging shift was about embracing this teaching, to sense encouragement from spirit and to step forward into fire's initiation.

Meanwhile, I missed Russia. In my mind's eye, when I turned my memory to Russia it became a memory that is the sound of ancient church bells pealing away in the distance – a mystical choir on the airwaves lulling me with the sound of Ave Maria. As the memory heightens, I bow in reverence to the varied colors of the wildflowers forming a quilt pattern across the landscape. I can visualize them bowing back, catching in the moment the glimmering essence of spirit as they shine out of this primordial land. How this wondrous land had captivated my soul!

Within the longing came a curious development. I received an invitation to return to Russia. I was being asked to come to Perm to participate in a family camp and to share some of my Shamanic teachings with the folks which were to attend. It would be the first time I would venture into this mysterious land alone. I, being the only foreigner, would have to teach through an interpreter. Did I have the strength to do this at a ten day camp? I could only hope so.

What I did know was that I was again going to Russia and indeed the journey was heating up! Ho!

Chapter 11 – Blessed by the Elementals

First family camp

I will come to you through thunder

I will come to you through rain

My sign will be the lightning

To make you whole again. M.W.

The Lesson:

After making the shift, the journey progresses into the first initiation

of fire – a blessing from the elementals.

Herons promise of regeneration brought with it the paradox of apprehension and excitement. This was a big act of power, both for myself and the Russian women organizers. It was also an act of deep trust and faith when as a group we would be plunged deeply into the unknown.

One of the most predominant figures in Russian folklore is the Firebird. This beautiful, mystical bird, with its fiery plumage, always appears during times of adversity when the hero of the story needs a helping hand. Little did we know our group would experience a visit from the Firebird in a rather unique form.

Soon I was off to Russia once more, taking the train from Moscow across the many miles and into the heart of Russia, to Perm. Upon my arrival I met Anna. She was an English student and would be my interpreter at camp. She was a petite, blonde, young woman who lived nearby with her sister and mother. My first thoughts were, "But she is so young!" I need not have been concerned. Anna is one of the many Russian sisters I have had the privilege of meeting who possesses the indomitable Russian spirit; overflowing with integrity, courage, and determination this bright, dedicated, young woman never faltered. Together we would forge both an intricate working partnership as well as becoming steadfast friends – grandmother and maiden working together to make camp a success and forever changing our view of how we perceived the world.

Soon, in a flurry of activity, preparations were in full swing as everyone made ready for camp. Food, clothing, bedding, materials, and sound systems all collected for our trek to the Urals. The day of departure had arrived. A huge mound of camp supplies, baggage, plus people were crammed into an ancient bus. In any act of power, however, one must first overcome several obstacles. First our ancient bus overheated and we had to wait for it to cool down. Travelling again, the bus finally stalled and would go no further. Striking off by foot we slowly made it to the Sylva River. There we had one more huge hurdle to overcome. Camp participants and our huge mound of luggage, food, and supplies had to cross the river by way of a small row boat.

The campsite was situated in a small enclosure nestled in a gentle bend in the river. Through a small stand of birch trees I could see two long, flat buildings which appeared to be dormitories. We made our way to the larger of the two, which also housed a large kitchen. Once inside my spirits plummeted. These old buildings, which at one time had been a sports camp, had lain unused for quite some time. Inside it smelt moldy, dusty, and totally derelict. My fellow Russian heroines have demonstrated to me over and over that there is nothing like faith and some good hard labor to transform a pig's ear into a silken purse. Out came mops, brooms, and pails of soapy water. Soon the whole building had been scrubbed down. I was then taken downstairs to the biggest transformation of all. The mess hall had been cleared and all of the tables and benches had been carried outside. Mattresses had instead been placed on the floor in a large area that was now screened off and covered with multicolored blankets. At the very end, one of the benches had been set up and draped, forming the camp altar.

Our group had decided earlier to set up the altar, depicting traditions of both the East and the West. It was now bedecked with wildflowers and pictures of Baba Ji, Jesus and Mother Mary, as well as pictures of Mary Magdalene and the Masters. With the adding of sage and sweet grass, representing the Shamanic tradition, the beautiful synthesis of spirit became complete. We had also decided to replicate this synthesis each day with our morning ceremony, opening with prayers and the casting of the circle through smudging, while another camp leader would then offer Eastern mantras.

Excitement mounted, as next morning camp was about to begin. Using the old metal flag pole out in front, one of the men clanged out the announcement to the forty participants attending. In casting the circle, I began with prayers and then the calling of the Four Directions, starting with the East, calling in the place of illumination; to the South, the place of looking close up; to the West, the home of the sacred dream and the feminine; and the North, the place of spirit. Calling to the Mother and the Father above, and our Mother Earth below, all connecting to the middle of the circle, to the heart, embracing us in full circle.

The Russians were enthralled. This was perhaps partly to have a foreigner in their midst, but again remember that for so long all things spiritual had been more inward. What had been kept alive had been done mainly through the grandmothers. To sit in sacred circle where we could freely honor the ancient Shamanic traditions of the land, coupled with the traditions they were bringing from the East, was beyond amazing and brought great joy.

Soon it was close to lunchtime. I went and sat outside, waiting for the lunch bell to ring. Suddenly I noticed clouds beginning to form on the horizon. Big, dark, ugly clouds billowed up and appeared to be coming closer. I watched, now fascinated with the rapidity of this approaching storm; the thunderclouds rolled and tumbled as they quickly descended upon us. Just as I was thinking I should take cover there was a blinding flash of lightning, accompanied by a deafening crack of thunder. A great bolt of lightning struck the flagpole, just several feet from where I was sitting.

What happened next was stranger still. The sky turned even more ominously dark, if that was possible, and wind arrived. In seconds the leaves on the surrounding trees were turned inside out as a spiral of wind came roaring in with the continuing thunder and lightning and proceeded to cleanse the entire campsite. Fire vigorously burned up all the old stagnant energy and then moved it out on the arms of spiral wind. A clean slate being prepared for our healing!

I sat there dumbstruck by the intensity of the energy. The air literally crackled with the lightning, the atmosphere sparkled with its aliveness. Suddenly I noticed my whole body beginning to heat up, to come alive. From the tips of my toes to the crown of my head I had suddenly come alive with intense heat. Spirit had come down to bless our camp, bringing with it this fiery experience.

We were to enter deeply into the teachings of fire. Fire is the most powerful element, often depicted as giving birth to the other elements (1). Upon looking back at this time I realize we were not only being blessed with fiery healing, but as this spark within each of us came alive our psychic awareness heightened, helping us to become open to fully collaborate with the subtle world (2). We were in spirit's workshop!

Our experience over the next several days was amazing. What I taught became incidental to the power of fire. Speaking from our hearts, feeling the heat of aliveness, our community came together in union. Each time we would get bogged down, heat would appear, and just like the tilting of a windmill, energy would transmute. Spirit would come, placing us always in the arms of the fiery experience. An incredible time of transformation! A lady later described feeling the heat so intensely that even the stone necklace she was wearing changed color.

Children also were not immune and showed a clarity and incredible depth of intuition. One youngster, only eight years old, explained the process he went through as he followed the meditation that was used for finding one's personal totem. He explained that he saw a dot on the horizon. He assumed this was a doorway or gate, and after he went through this it was okay. He was then able to get in touch with his own power animal.

During our fiery experience, several women approached me asking if we could hold a women's circle. These first women's circles would become a precursor to future developments in the journey. In response to their request we held two very different circles. The first came from concern the women held for their families. Women worried about the health of their families, as well as the very grave economic hardships each of the families faced. They also worried about their sons and the real threat of being conscripted into the army. Often sons would be thrown into schooling they weren't very interested in, simply to avoid this threat. It was interesting to note that in working with the children I found the girls all wanted more empowerment in their lives, whereas the boys, regardless of age, all wanted peace.

The first circle was a circle of prayer. Casting a circle to create a sacred container we then placed our prayers in the center. Once the prayers were in the center we then did an exercise with sound, where energy given through sound would then send our prayers to spirit.

The next circle had a very different purpose. It was to help women share their experience with each other and to talk about how difficult it was just to live out each day. Again we opened the circle by calling the Four Directions and honoring the ancestors, especially calling the grandmothers who had gone before us to bring us their wisdom. I spoke of women's power and what that meant for each of them.

Immediately, one of the women spoke out in a loud and abrupt voice. She basically said that what I had to understand, as a foreigner, was that in Russia a woman always stood behind her man. That was the way it had always been and that was the way it would always be. I was shocked by this outburst. Inwardly my thought was if that was really what they all felt, then this was indeed going to be a short group.

Unsure of how to proceed after this bombshell, I simply began telling them about a woman I admired very much. She was Russian and her name was Helena Roerich. She had dedicated her life to writing and encouraging women to become empowered. In preparation for the writing of the *Agni Yoga* volumes the Masters had taken Helena through an intense process of fiery transmutation. She literally became "a walker between the worlds"; on one hand to be in the physical world, but to also communicate with the Masters in the subtle world, to travel to the far-off worlds. In her writings, Helena wrote about a time called the new era, when the Feminine Principles would again be reclaimed. In honor of this remarkable woman I very simply began to read some quotes from her writing.

"Where women are revered and safeguarded, prosperity reigns and the Gods rejoice. The new epoch under the rays of Uranus will bring the renaissance of women. The Epoch of Maitreya is the Epoch of the Mother of the World."

"Woman was the chosen link between the two worlds – the visible and the invisible. We must always deepen our knowledge of Mother Nature. Woman must not only defend her own rights but free thought for all of humanity… We, as Mother, Grandmother, are life giver, life protector; let us also become Mother the leader, all giver, all receiver."

"Woman is the personification of nature – and it is nature that teaches man, not man nature. Women are guardians of sacred knowledge. Welfare of state rests firmly upon the foundation of family." (3)

As I went on to describe this truly remarkable woman, I said how I believed that she had truly given us a gift, in that she provided us with such a strong model for fiery achievement. With that, the energy within the circle magically began to shift and change. Soon women began to talk about their lives and just how difficult these last few years had been since the economic collapse. They simply began to speak from their heart. Given the earlier outburst, the shift was almost like a miracle.

Women spoke about grave alcohol abuse that they witnessed in their families, often leading to violence or desertion by their spouses.

Most women were single parents, so had to be not only the head of the household, but act as the bread-winner in the family. Many were trapped in horrific situations where they had to watch their mates slowly drink themselves to oblivion every day, but because of complex laws around housing subsidies, were unable to leave. Slowly it began to dawn on them just how strong they really were. As the women shared collectively, they began to gain more confidence. They also began expressing themselves from a place of power rather than subservience.

We finished off the circle with dance movement, inviting them to imagine that they were wild women similar to their primordial ancestors, grounded and connected to the energy of the land. With this strength and connection they did not need to bow down to anyone or to be afraid. We began to dance, and as the music lifted them into this primal energy, each of the women began to come alive. Smiling, laughing, and chanting to that ancient space within, they began to naturally celebrate – to come truly alive. They later shared that the circle was taken down to the river where they each made flower crowns prior to going into the river to swim. They said it made them feel like queens. These women had gleaned a sense of hope from the writings of Helena Roerich and had come alive. Sacred fire coupled with reconnection to the Earth, that primal energy once again came alive and gave birth to a strong and empowered self, now ready to be expressed as the new story.

Perhaps the women of Russia, all women, could begin to step into leadership – something the Russian women were already doing in their homes and with their families. Just maybe, with the birth of the wild woman in each of us, we no longer need to stand behind our man, but side by side, bringing in balance for the new paradigm, bringing back the wisdom that lives deep in the wild woman in us all.

There were so many unique experiences – from the beautiful braiding of flower wreaths, to the soul touching Russian singing. It all provided a magnificent tapestry, suspending us for ten days in our fiery workshop of spirit.

May the journey continue. Ho!

Left: Storyteller, Nicholi Shadowev Right: Roerich Museum

Dark shadows surface, swirling deep

Destroy the promise, faith to keep. M.W.

The Lesson:

Having gone through intense initiation, and before progressing

further on the journey, the student is tested for strength and depth of sincerity – often experienced as the opposite of the light-filled initiation.

After camp finished I had arranged to go back to the Altai in Siberia. As you may remember, Ludmila had encouraged me to remember Zvenigorod. This mystery in mind, I hoped to visit this tiny village where the Roerichs had spent time prior to going on their Altai-Himalaya journey. The adventure that I now recount truly supports the saying that truth is often stranger than fiction.

I would go through an experience of what I call backlash. People often experience this as part of their process of integration. That is, one gets to visit the opposite energy of their initiation.

"There is an obscure law in Nature which produces this rather curious result, that whenever there is a great outrush of higher and grander forces, there is also a corresponding efflux of undesirable energy." (1)

Galina was unable to accompany me to the Altai. She suggested instead that I join a young newly married couple, Igor and Natasha, who wanted to travel along with the groom's sister, Olga, into the Altai for their honeymoon. I had met Igor at the Healing Summit the summer before. My first instinct was that this was a rather unusual arrangement, but as Natasha was said to speak English I dismissed my own concerns. Promise of a visit to an old storyteller and then

105

travel to Uimon, the village where the Roerichs had stayed, overrode my doubts. There was a museum in this village dedicated to the Roerichs and I looked forward to learning more.

As I made ready to leave, little did I know that I would soon be facing a series of challenges which would push me to the very limits of my endurance. Backlash is similar to coming up against a huge wall while spirit stands by as you search for the opening, the key which will let you through. It becomes not only a test of faith, but also a battle of will where you must challenge once again the old conditioning, complete with your old fears. There seems always a critical time within the journey where one is given a truly difficult obstacle. In essence it became an aspect of the fiery dance of initiation, where I was given the opportunity to dance through the darkness, looking through an obscure maze for the light.

While travelling by bus to Gorno-Altaisk I soon discovered, contrary to what I had been promised, that Igor and his sister Olga spoke almost no English and Natasha very little. Upon arrival, plans too had changed. Rather than staying with Galina's daughter, we were now to go now to Igor's friends and stay there until we could hire a car.

The couple tried to welcome us, but it soon became obvious that things here were very strange. Swirling chaos seemed to surround us. While the two men talked, the two girls and I got to sit and wait...

and wait... and wait. While we waited the lady of the house indicated I should go over to the bathroom and look inside.

As soon as she opened the door a small crack I saw a frenetic blur of movement in the shape of a huge dog, snarling, growling and snapping as it lunged against the door. It seems the couple where we were staying had a vicious dog for a pet. This was my warning not to go near it.

To make matters worse, the house seemed dirty and neglected, and there appeared to be no food whatever. Finally we were able to have some tea, by which time I was exhausted. I was shown into a room off the main hall, where the young girls and I would sleep. I had just laid my head down when the door burst open and the hostess arrived, bringing all of her jewelry for us to look at. We admired the jewelry her husband had made. Due to our language barrier I was unsure of the purpose of showing us the jewelry and asked the hostess if she wished to sell it. This made our hostess very angry and a great uproar ensued.

The commotion brought everyone into the room. Suddenly it was decided there would be a concert. Why in my room, I am not sure. People continued to talk after the concert and finally the girls and I, begging that we were exhausted, persuaded Igor and the couple to leave. The party continued on, just outside the room, and amidst barking, growling, and loud talking, I finally drifted off into a very troubled and restless sleep.

Next day, no one wanted to move. Finally it was decided that the young girls and I would go to the museum just across the road and Igor would go to make arrangements to hire a car. We wandered around the museum. Again I was drawn to the ancient Shaman's drum I had seen in my previous visit. What really intrigued me was the back of the drum. About two thirds of the way up the back of the drum was a stick that went across and this was intersected by another stick going from the top to the bottom of the drum. At the top, the drum had a diamond shaped face carved in primitive fashion. The horizontal stick had ribbons of different colors tied to it. This ancient drum radiated a strong and beautiful energy, even through the glass.

After viewing the exhibits we again waited for Igor, to no avail. To date, our whole trip had centered on waiting for Igor and I was beginning to lose my temper. Back at the apartment Igor finally breezed in, saying we wouldn't be leaving today, but travel arrangements had been finalized. Meanwhile our hosts had invited their son over for an evening of storytelling.

Once gathered together, they all began trying to persuade me not to attempt travelling to Uimon. They said some hostilities had surfaced in this village between the Old Believers and the Roerich followers and they felt it would not be safe to travel there. Curiously, the storytelling took place in the middle of the hallway, under an electrical dome which was supposed to bring healing. Storytelling over, I went back to my room. Two days with very little food had put me at low ebb.

108

Next a new tactic began. As I sat and read in my room, someone would appear every few minutes, coming to recount the horrors they felt I would face should I attempt the journey. The stories ranged from overt violence to the likelihood of older women being raped. In the midst of the stories, the dog got loose and began attacking my closed door, making it sound as though a rabid beast was about to burst in. Once the dog was restrained, our host rushed into my room shouting at me that if I were to continue I would likely be threatened with rape, as older women were in grave danger.

The whole experience was getting ridiculous. Soon, however, fear began to creep in. How would I get them to leave and worse yet – what if they just left without me? I sat up all night and prayed – praying with all of my strength to be delivered from this strange, chaotic environment. It was hot and stuffy, and as I was beginning day three with little sleep and hardly any food, fear began to get the upper hand; in fact, it had become magnified. I had the strangest feeling that I was somehow going to be dumped and left with no idea where I was, no idea how I would negotiate my way back, even to Novosibirsk.

Around five in the morning my fears got the better of me. I now heard movement outside my room, as if they were getting ready to leave. I went out to confront them. At this point I totally lost it, made worse by our host laughing at me. I decided at that point that I would become like a bloodhound. That is, everywhere they went I would go with them. It turned out, however, that once we were outside walking and the fierce dog calmed down, I realized my fears were greatly exaggerated. We were indeed going to the river, as they had said.

It was cool and peaceful down there, and I managed to do a ceremony in honor of the spirits of place, asking them for protection on this journey to such a sacred valley. With the ceremony complete, the energy appeared to lighten somewhat. As we packed to leave, Igor had again disappeared. Thirty minutes elapsed when the man of the house discovered that Igor had somehow gotten locked in the bathroom. By this time I was beginning to wonder if drug taking was involved.

Arriving at the bus station, we had no need to worry about getting a car. There were many drivers waiting to be hired. Igor really hadn't made any previous transport arrangements – there was no need. We were on our way into the valley. The driver was local and seemed friendly enough. I was so relieved to be travelling again. Igor was sick and throwing up, something that would be a constant throughout our travels. The landscape unfolded before us, an intricate patchwork of beauty as hill upon hill created a feast for the eyes, doing much to restore my exhausted and depleted soul.

As we rounded the corner on the highway, my first view of the Katun came into view. What an incredible river it was – this mighty river upon whose banks the final battle between good and evil, between brother and brother, would be fought. To see this ribbon of magic pushing forward between the banks of earth, casting a presence of energy in the patchwork landscape, it was not hard to imagine the river's amazing destiny.

Soon our driver pulled off the main road and we took a turn towards a small village called Mendur-Sokkon where we would stay the night. Just before entering the village we stopped before what appeared to be a natural stone doorway to the village. The driver explained that it was their custom to honor this place before going down into the village. Getting out of the car and finding a small piece of cloth to add to the others already there, I went over to pay my respects.

Inside the village we pulled up beside one of the small houses where an elderly couple came out to greet us. They appeared to be in their seventies and both smiled a big welcome. The old woman disappeared briefly, coming out carrying a small bowl filled with white liquid, explaining that we were all to drink from this bowl. It was filled with fermented mare's milk. This is a welcoming custom of the Altai peoples.

Greetings over, the storyteller now took us to where we were to stay overnight, and then on to the museum which he had recently developed. We walked over to the entrance of the museum and I immediately felt heat surge through my body. He asked if we had felt anything and explained that the reaction was due to the prayer ties said to be one hundred years old which were exhibited just inside the door of the museum. He invited us to ask questions, so I asked about the meaning of the back of the drum I had seen in the museum in Gorno-Altaisk.

He proceeded to tell me that the face on the back of the drum represented the ancestors and was in honor of them. This was always at the top of the drum. The horizontal stick with the tie rags on it represented the various cosmic connections of the drum's owner. The tie rags, with different colors, symbolized the Earth, the stars, totems, and so on. The face at the top of the drum was a constant reminder to honor our Old Ones, the ancestors. He spoke of the spirit of the Altai being masculine, and that of Om Mai feminine, with balance always between the two.

It was such an honor to meet the old storyteller; a much needed reprieve from my chaotic journey. The reprieve continued. Igor had disappeared, but Natasha and Olga made supper and, gratefully, I got to sleep in a warm, clean bed.

Next day everyone had disappeared, as well as the food, and while I had been out someone had searched my luggage. Things seemed to be deteriorating again. As we were about to leave, the old man's niece appeared looking very angry, demanding more money (I would later discover it was money owed to her by Igor for some antlers he had bought). Then the driver demanded more money, apparently not as yet having received any. Reluctantly I handed over more money and we left.

We moved now towards the valley of Mount Beluhka. The energy of the mountains was palpable. This was a very ancient land. Bits of old crumbling rock pierced its way through the gentle, soft, rolling mountain sides. We continued to climb, moving higher and higher, going up through what was called the Croweliski Gate or Pass. We then began our descent, moving down into Mount Beluhka valley.

Soon we were in the town of Cocksa and stopped for lunch. Again I was confronted with more bad news. After saying they now had no money and I was to pay for everyone's lunch, they also informed me they had left Galina's instructions behind, so we would have to move on to Uimon. I agreed and said nothing. I had a strong sense that once I confronted what was really going on, our trip would be over.

We were now travelling along the mighty Katun River. The mountains were even more spectacular as we approached Uimon. It was like we were driving into the center of a huge bowl, the tiny village completely ringed by a circle of mountains reminded me of cup and saucer – the village being the cup, nestled in the strong protection of the saucer shaped mountains.

We arrived at the village museum to find it closed. Tensions seemed high. Many of the villagers would just turn away and refuse to speak to us. Angry voices could be heard everywhere. *"Brother against brother on the Katun."*(2) Energy seemed almost at the boiling point. We walked down the street and out of the corner of my eye I noticed a very tall man in a straw hat standing perfectly still in the middle of his garden. The others in my party had already passed and I, pausing to catch my breath, looked over at the garden where the man stood. As I looked over he took off his hat and made a deep bow in honor of my arrival. Suddenly it struck me that this had all been an illusion and I was now coming to the end of the test! That deep bow seemed to be saying to me, "Well you made it. You have come through the challenge and all is well."

Meanwhile, our driver had found the manager of the museum, and we could stay at her place for the night. As we approached the museum the driver brought the car to a stop and my companions said we needed to pay the driver. Confused, I said, "But I have already paid." In the moment, I totally lost it. We began yelling at each other, with me yelling, "How often do I have to pay for this ride?" They also insisted it was to cost more money to get a ride back. The cost had now surpassed the cost of airfare from Moscow to Siberia!

At that moment, the lady that ran the museum had arrived. She must have thought we were all crazy, especially the foreigner, as by now I was screaming like a mad banshee. Everyone was angry and frustrated, including the driver. He proceeded dumping our entire luggage by the side of the road. I finally agreed to payment, but said there would be no more money – we would have to make our return trip another way.

The driver drove off in a huff and we turned our attention now on the curator of the Roerich museum. Her name was Lubov. In the Icon of the Sophia there are the three muses – faith is Vera, hope is Nadia or Mezda, and Lubov is love. I was standing in front of love. She was surrounded with light and became a huge relief for this travel weary foreigner. In fact, things would be fine, as the challenge was indeed over. Lubov would provide us with the first real meal in days, and also help us to get a ride back to Gorno-Altaisk.

She took us to see the museum. The exterior of the museum had been carved by artists from all over the country. The shutters on each of the windows had exquisite symbols depicting the Roerichs carved into the light colored wood.

Lubov was part of the Agni Yoga group in the village. She explained that there was a conflict between their group and the Old Believers that had come out of an unusual distortion. There had been an article in the paper suggesting the Roerich group had been accused of drinking blood in their rituals. Nothing could have been further from the truth and it was curious how such a strange conflict had started. As tension flared, Lubov had to close the museum.

In the museum were wonderful exhibits of Roerich's pictures and maps depicting their Altai-Himalayan journey. Lubov went on to say that the Roerichs stayed at the village for approximately two weeks and were very highly regarded by the people of the area. Nicholas and Helena spent their days exploring the beautiful landscape and rocky structures of the countryside. At the end of her talk Lubov said very simply, "This is what the Roerichs envisioned as the future town of Russia. This is Zvenigorod, the City of the Bells!"

Legend of the City of the Bells tells of a future town, some say one that already exists in the subtle world and that it will one day appear in this area, bringing fruition to Russia's great spiritual destiny.

"Katun is welcoming. The Blue Mountains are resonant. White is Belukha. The flowers are vivid and the green grasses and cedars are calming. Who said the Altai is cruel and unapproachable? Whose heart has become fearful of the austere power and beauty? On the 17th of August we beheld Belukha. It was so clear and reverberant. Verily, Zvenigorod!" (3)

Not only had I met the challenge of the test and come through, I had been given this mystical glimpse of the real Russia. Encouraged by this added information, it was exciting to think of now moving forward.

May the journey continue. Ho!

Chapter 13 – Mask Making

Mask Making

I call them the winged Ones, messengers of joy

Of hope and of beauty, up there in the sky. M.W.

The Lesson:

A Shaman's mask helps arouse inner fire, connecting the student to

past and future and all around – ultimately, lessons of oneness.

Remembering the intense backlash, I knew my Russian sisters and I had achieved a huge act of power. Now we were about to launch another. After the fiery experiment of the summer before, I had word in the spring from Anna. She had been contacted by some of the kids from the previous summer camp and they wanted me to come and be with them in camp again. It seemed the journey was once again pushing me forward. Summer arrived and soon I along with two other Canadian women were on our way to Russia.

Agni Yoga reminds us that joy, courage, and endurance nourishes the inner fire (1). As our two small groups of women from East and West made plans once again to join, we certainly demonstrated these attributes – especially joy – like the winged ones who heralded our journey from overhead. To achieve another huge act of power was beyond exciting.

This time we would be travelling by train to Kindelino. There were about eighty people at camp and the theme this year was about connection. It was decided we would all make masks. All participants, including the young children, would make and decorate a mask.

The tradition of the Shaman's mask is as ancient as Shamanism itself. As well as a tool that fosters empowerment, there were often unique masks created specifically as a means of strengthening the Shaman's healing powers. I once had a student who, upon completing her mask, stepped into an unusual persona of power. The moment she put on her mask she would become an ancient male Japanese Healer. He was very fierce. The transformation was very dramatic, giving her healing gifts that were quite incredible.

The mask has the power to help the novice tap into the wisdom aspect of themselves, to the inner feminine, ultimately empowering both women and men alike. Participants are taken through Shamanic journeying. Through this process they receive guidance as to what the mask or new face will be. It becomes a profound experience of releasing the old story and stepping into the new. As the mask facilitates the arousal of inner fire, it brings in the knowledge of both past and future (2). In this way it contributes to balance, healing, and strength, yet always brings the student back to the present, to one's center with heart. The Mayan tradition calls this new story the Era of the Flower and Agni Yoga refers to the symbol of the flower as spiritual knowledge or spiritual perfection. Spirit is the spark that ignites our soul – a flame which intensifies our life force and thus becomes fire. Making a mask assists in this process.

As the days at camp moved forward the masks for each participant took form. The final days were spent decorating the individual masks, and those who wished could also do their own personal ceremony, where they would leave their masks out overnight connecting their new face to the Earth.

We would also have a very special ceremony about "one." When we put on our masks our faces became hidden behind the persona each of us had chosen for the mask. All boundaries, nationalities, and faith became blurred. We just became one. It became a remarkable exercise in community.

As well as focusing on oneness, I also wanted to honor the connection of our small group of leaders from East and West. To do this I had made up a set of three bundles for each of us. A bundle, in the traditional sense, is the sacred bundle of the Shaman and is usually called the medicine bag. It usually contains the articles of power a Shaman has accumulated over their years of training. Marie-Lu-Lorler noted that these bundles seen in all cultures always carried many of the same items – tobacco, herbs, stones, animal talismans such as skin or fur, teeth, bones, and often a sacred pipe. (3)

There are other kinds of bundles however, which can be utilized as a means to connect or to honor. Remember the bundle I had presented to the reluctant Shaman of Lake Teletskoe. I did this to honor his wisdom. I wished to present bundles now to the camp organizers as a way of honoring our unique connection and our joint act of power.

The sets of bundles were based on Helena Roerich's writing. In her writing she spoke of the ancient days and a land called Gotl, where the priestess' brought forth the Feminine Principle in all things. The temples of this special land were symbolized by thread for the hearth, string as the calling of deity, and the serpent as knowledge. In the old days the temples, which were said to be circular in style, became the trinity of the Temple of the Moon, Temple of the Sun, and Temple of the Serpent. (4)

I created two sets of bundles to symbolize the ancient temples. One set I kept in Canada, the second I gave to the Russian women to keep. I hoped it was a way to strengthen our connection, but also to encourage empowerment for all in our future acts of power.

Soon it was the last day in camp. On this final morning we again honored the Four Directions and smudged, as we had done each day. Suddenly the energy shifted and changed in the circle. This strong yet subtle energy, both serene yet exuberant, flowed through and around us in the circle. No one wanted to leave. I could clearly sense the energy, but there were several in the circle who could actually see radiant light that was embracing our entire circle. It would give us a brief preview of our future collaboration with spirit.

Evening came and it was time to gather in our final circle. We began to exchange gifts. As a part of this exchange I had brought three deerskin hand-drums to give away. Deer is the totem seen as the symbol for gentleness and heart. When becoming drum it mirrors the heartbeat of Mother Earth; Her heart, our heart, all connecting in a harmony of one. We were ending camp and the lessons of "one," but how difficult it was to leave. Although we did not experience the intensity of fire as in the first camp, we did experience much about loving community and heart. It had been a short ten days, but connections had gone deep, carving tender places in our hearts.

As the hour grew late, sadly it was time for us Canadians to leave. The first leg of our journey took us by boat across the river. Everyone gathered there to say goodbye. The boat began to slide through the feather-like mist, now swirling up from the surface of the water, and a fine drizzle of rain had begun to fall. Voices saying, "We love you," echoed across the mist, echoing our special connection. Sadness and joy welled up together, making us full, making our magical camp complete.

May the teachings of the journey continue. Ho!

Chapter 14 – Connection to the Land

Connection to the land

Our Lady fair, in caverns deep

Brings us the light, our dreams She keeps

She is the grail, the Rose, our lesson

Lighting mysteries now, to new heart vision. M.W.

The Lesson:

The student, having been blessed by the elementals and undergone arousal of fire with the mask, now moves onward to lessons of heart.

These lessons are built on a solid foundation of land and traditions. When a student makes a profound connection to the land and ancient wisdom, they begin to see beauty. Through cognizance of beauty their hearts begin to open.

Within Shamanic tradition the world is viewed as being somewhat like a layer cake. In simple terms there is an upper, lower, and middle world, and the student strives to journey to these worlds – especially the upper world, which is the realm of fire. To achieve this, the student must learn the lessons of heart.

In Agni Yoga the teachings of heart is called Surya Vidya, meaning fiery and centrality (1). Agni Yoga describes our physical body as the solar plexus being the antechamber; the kundalini, the laboratory; the brain and centers, the estates; and finally the heart, the central temple. The heart thinks, discerns, affirms, and unifies. This central temple gives us our highest form of communion. (2)

At this stage of my journey I didn't understand or know this. I was merely being guided to appreciate a connection to the Earth, to go deeper in building an earthly foundation. On the outer edges of my perception came a faint glimmering of knowing that my journey was now helping me discover a whole new rhythm.

There is an automatic deepening of connection when travelling in a country where the people there refer to the land as Mother. Mother

Russia is vast, encompassing nine time zones, and throughout this, connection is apparent. This is especially so in places like the Altai where connection and honoring of the land has been uninterrupted.

I travelled into the Altai many times during the course of my journey and each time I could sense myself stepping into that unique place of wonder. How does one describe a journey into the Altai? How does one speak of the magical voice of the Altai? A music that resonates with one's heart, a thread of melody that says simply, *come*. Sound similar to the ancient melody of the throat singers, ringing out pure and clear in one's heart. Unfolding before one's eyes, the rolling hills that gives rise to mountains which give rise to sky. All dappled in the vibrant color of purity; a place that is like a great magnet, calling all who know the way to come. Come to join in the reverence so deeply felt by the Altai people. A place that means "my God" or "Kahn Altai" (my native God) to the Altai people.

It was customary to stop at the border and make an offering to the spirits of place prior to travelling into the Altai. On one such occasion, after we had made our offering and were once more back on the bus, I asked my Russian companions to share their impressions about Altai. One felt that the beauty of nature fed her soul and because of the special energy there, one always felt better. She thought perhaps it was because of the ancient, pagan lineage in the Altai that included a great respect for nature. Another said that for her, Belukha (Russia's holy mountain) with its pristine white peaks was symbolic of purity and became an example to us all, teaching us about what to strive for at an inner level. She described Belukha as a great temple, matching with the inner temple that lived within each of us. She was enthralled by Her beauty. Galina's sister was delighted with the great beauty of the Altai, but was more drawn to the Katun River – the great river whose source begins at Mount Belukha. In talking about the valley, I too remembered stories that had been shared with me about this special place where the land seemed alive with mystical energy. Local villagers tell of the old village Elders who can remember a time when holy people lived in the Cock Su Mountains. Their community was a secret place. They also told me of a strange woman appearing one day. During her brief stay in the village, she picked up a candle and said, "Be careful with electricity." Then she left. Some time later there was a fire at the church, but not nearly as bad as it could have been had they not had warning. They also spoke of the children having encounters with men and women dressed in brightly colored clothing not in a style of the area. At first the children were afraid but agreed to meet, in fact, several times. The strangers talked mostly about what was a good way to live. Like on Lake Teletskoe, they had witnessed unusual light phenomena and a Healer reported being out walking one day when she came to a cave. Before her eyes the cave shape-shifted into an ornate temple. She closed her eyes and looked again, but the temple was still there. The energy in the area is indeed mysterious.

After travelling many miles along the Katun River, we arrived in the area of Tyungoor. This was the place that would take us to a place known to the people of the Altai as the Sacred Field, home of the ancient Babas. Upon arriving we made our way up a steep embankment. These ancient Babas stood on a large plateau or plain high above. The plain was nestled against high hills which cupped the land in chalice formation, seemingly holding the place untouched, shrouded in silent beauty as it had for hundreds of years. We were indeed on holy ground!

Silently walking through the tall grass and flowers I came upon my first Baba. It was hard to imagine that it stood before me as it had done on this plateau for over a thousand years. The stones in this area seemed mostly male. Their primitive faces carved into the rock were still quite distinctive. The height of each stone averaged between three and four feet high. As I kneeled down to pay homage to this old Baba I felt a special energy that radiated from the area, making one tingle and feel totally alive.

After holding a circle to honor the spirits of place and placing prayer ties on the natural altar nearby, I then made my way to some huge stones lying on the perimeter of the field. Maria, a local Shaman we were to meet later, had told us that these large rocks were healing rocks. They were oblong in shape, flat on top, and stood well over eight feet high. With help, I clambered up to the top of one of the stones and lay down on its flat granite surface. I was immediately lulled into a sense of deep peace and my inner vision became filled with a brilliant orange color. Another introduction to the elemental fiery energy.

Slowly I made my way back through the field, honoring each of the Baba stones that were scattered across the field. Suddenly I noticed movement and realized I had a very special escort. Many, many salamanders were walking with me, affirming the fiery energy of this ancient place. The lizard, or salamander, in Shamanic tradition is symbolic of fire; they are unique in that they are said to be able to regenerate their own limbs. Research has indicated that the energy of the salamander is similar to that of Shamans.

Some time after my first trip to Russia, a friend from Glastonbury suggested I read a special book. It was called *Prophecy of the Russian Epic – How the Holy Mountains Released the Mighty Russian Heroes From Their Rocky Caves*, written by Sergei Prokofieff (3). The book was a translation of an old Russian epic or bylina, meaning long poem. It had first been given in the oral tradition and later written, telling of the fearful trials endured by the Russian people and their ensuing battle to overcome these trials. The epic describes the Russian heroes being locked deep in the mountain, but finally being freed. As the story unfolds, the Russian heroes are forgiven for their misdeeds by the angelic forces, but then given the test of staying awake. Only one hero, named Ilya, succeeds, and has to face the dark forces alone. Going into fierce battle, he is soon exhausted and is in great fear of being unable to succeed. (4)

"…Ukya falls to the moist Mother Earth, that is he turns through mediation of light, reflected by the Russian Earth of the Mother of God, to the forces of the cosmic sphere of Mary – Sophia! …With this Ilya is able to rise to the next stage – to the listening heart." (5)

Within this epic, the Sophia is always referred to as "our moist Mother Earth." To many Russians the Earth and the Divine Sophia are one and the same. It would seem that Russian people intuitively know that the Russian land reflects light or rays of energy radiated from the cosmos. This light is then absorbed and reflected from the land itself, ultimately bringing consciousness to the people living there. Perhaps because of this it is often said that when a Russian wishes to pray, to reach spirit, they look down rather than casting their gaze skyward. They reach down to the hallowed land and look down to the Earth because to honor the Earth is to honor spirit. In Russia, Earth is seen as the Great Mother's sister.

I would continuously experience this understanding and profound connection to the Earth, which in turn deepened my own connection throughout my journey. In fully opening to the beauty of the land, I became aware of the subtle tug at my heart.

What was happening on the journey can be most touchingly illustrated in a ceremony I witnessed. A group of us were travelling in the Tulkva valley, in the Baikal region, and were told we were being taken to a special ceremony in honor of the thirty-three mountains there. The mountains were said to be thirty-three warriors of Gesser Kahn who had been turned into mountains and now they blessed and watched over the area. The valley was also alive with the water of some two hundred springs, each said to have special healing qualities for different parts of the body.

We arrived at a shrine where the ceremony would take place; the Old Man arrived also. He had a name, but Old Man is what he preferred to be called. He had begun doing the ceremony in 1990. He said he decided that, "Every stupid man knows how to pray for himself, but now he could pray for others." We gathered with him outside the temple. The energy in the area was extremely strong and seemed to pulse through one's body. He told us the ceremony would take about two and a half hours. He would be offering tea, then vodka to each of the Masters of the Mountains. As he did this he asked my friend Galina, who was our interpreter, if she would continuously call out the names of each person in our party as a special prayer for our safe journey on their land. Then he took the remaining contents in the cup and did special prayers for both Alhon Island and Lake Baikal. His final prayers went to honor the fire – Agni Yoga.

It was deeply moving to watch this Old Man carry out his ceremony to the spirits of the mountains with both reverence and caring. He stood out in the blazing sun for at least two and a half hours praying to the spirits of the mountains. I was struck once again by the deep care and connection grassroots Siberian people have to both the Earth and to the sacred.

A profound, deep connection to the beauty of the land coupled with the wisdom of the Elders, was giving me the needed lessons of heart.

These lessons were propelling me forward to a new rhythm called "the listening heart."

May the journey continue. Ho!

Top: Valentin in ceremony
Bottom left: Black Shaman Basil
Bottom right: Shaman's Rock

Great Eagle deigns to look at me,

He questions if I have the right

To enter his abode of light. M.W.

The Lesson:

Oneness gives birth through a profound connection to the land and the ancient Shamanic traditions are what give meaning to that connection. In honoring the Earth traditions, the journey provides a solid foundation upon which to receive the teachings of heart and fire.

Thus it was to the Shamanic traditions that my journey would next take me. In the earlier years it had been difficult to meet Shamans. Things were not yet open and often you were taken to those who were merely called "old men" or "old women." Now it was easier, so after the second camp I travelled to the Lake Baikal region hoping to meet some Shamans.

Lake Baikal is the largest body of fresh water in the world, possessing unique species of life forms including fresh water seals. On the north side of the lake was Shaman's Rock, situated off Alhon Island. This had long been a place of initiation for Shamans. People of this area predominately followed the Shamanic traditions. On the south side of the lake there seemed to be a mixture of both Shamanic and Buddhist traditions.

It was on the south side that I began the journey. Here I would meet a Shaman who told me he was of the black tradition. His name was Vasily or Basil. At one time Basil had been a school teacher. He had five brothers and their father did not want any of them to become Shamans. Tragically, four of his brothers died, one right after the other. In desperation Basil went to Mongolia, to the Shaman's center to gain protection against his family's misfortune. Reluctantly Basil became a black Shaman. He explained that being a black or white Shaman had nothing to do with good or evil, but rather was determined by the gifts of the Shamans. It is believed that there are fifty-five Gods that are white and forty-four that are black. When you are a black Shaman you are able to ward off evil or curses, but if you are a white Shaman you are able to work with the fifty-five white Gods only. Basil was a black Shaman, meaning that he was able to work with both white and black Gods.

Next day Basil planned to take us to the sacred springs and shrines unique to the area. Here he would demonstrate a healing and cleansing. Upon arrival at the sacred spring he put forth his prayers, asking us to do this also. He requested that I kneel down in front of the spring while doing so, explaining that, like him, I was connected to the sun and this was my source of energy as a Shaman. As a part of his ceremonial costume he wore a large bronze disc around his neck. Then, taking a mouthful of vodka, he proceeded to spray it across my back. He did this four times. The custom was to do it three times, but he wanted to be thorough. He then presented me with blessed grain which I was to spread in the corners and closets of my home to complete the cleanse. The feeling of rejuvenation was remarkable!

134

The Russian people connect to the Earth, to their dear Mother Russia, as well as honoring the divine plan of the cosmos, the great synthesis of within, without, above and below. They have the ability to honor all great teachers, yet retain respect for their old Shamanic ways in which both ancestors and nature are seen as sacred. I expressed my gratitude to Basil and as we continued our journey I hoped I would learn more about the old Shamanic ways.

By chance, I would later meet a young Altai woman who also spoke of the black and white Shamanic traditions as she understood them. She emphasized that there was usually a genetic link, and for women it was only after they were married and had children that they would be ready to become Shamans. She explained that there is usually some illness which occurs that cannot be understood and the relatives will then take that person to a Shaman – one powerful enough to work with both light and dark energies, hence strong enough to open the person's centers.

The young woman went on to tell us a story of a young girl from Gorno-Altaisk who got married, had two sons, and then quite inexplicably became completely disabled with a disease of the spine. One day the woman was home alone when she had a vision where three angels appeared. Each angel wore a different colored dress – pink, blue, and one black. The angels told the young woman she was on the verge of death and it was time. Suddenly, the black angel struck her on the spine. The young Healer was so surprised she jumped. Now once again able to move, she quickly recovered and returned to work.

A short time later, while attending a meeting at work, a curious thing happened. She could see the internal organs of everybody attending the meeting. She thought she must be going crazy, so went home. Once home, however, she realized she had be given the gift of healing. That is, she had experienced the visions of a medical intuitive. This, coupled with the use of smoke from juniper, used for treatment information, this young woman has become a gifted Healer. This is a legacy she feels was passed down from her Altai mother and her grandfather.

Next we would travel to the northern side of Lake Baikal. We were to meet a Shaman by the name of Valentin. He was quite unique in that he had a PhD in Comparative Religions and had published a book about the similarities of different religions. He also had three thumbs. In his region, only those people with an extra bone in their body were said to qualify as Shamans. Thus his community had asked him to be their next Shaman.

Valentin was a tall dark man and very handsome – thought to be an ancestor of Ghengis Khan. As well as his interest in different religions, he also had a gift for writing poetry and much of his Shamanic work came through his poetry. Once we arrived first at Elantsy, his home village, we were driven out onto a high plateau to see the community's sacred tree. The plateau consisted of rocky terrain, windswept and barren. Their ancestral tree was a birch tree, growing out of the heart of a very large stone. Like most Shamanic traditions their sacred tree was symbolic of the Tree of Life, encompassing the upper, middle, and lower worlds. They also honored the elements and what seemed common to all traditions was the special attention and honoring placed on fire. In their tradition the Elders, upon death, were placed on the fire so they could then fly. It was here at the tree that Valentin had been initiated into his tribe as a Shaman.

Their clan went back for five centuries and as Valentin said, "If we are deserving, there will be a sixth." They had continued being nomads until the 1920s. When asked why they travelled, an old woman replied that, "This was natural, as everything moved in the cosmos. The Earth moves, the stars move and so we must dance with them. We all move together."

Throughout the Baikal in ancient times, hitching posts had been erected, symbolic of the Tree of Life. These posts had been carved into four segments, the top of which looked like a flame and represented the polar, or North Star, the next segment was the upper world, the third the middle world, and the one at the very bottom the lower world.

During the years of repression of Shamanic practices these hitching posts had all but disappeared. One day, so the story goes, an old Elder had a dream and in the dream he was told by the ancestors that

137

people must once again build the hitching posts. Otherwise, said the ancestor, from the other side it is difficult to travel to you on my white horse, as there are no posts to tie up to. With the advent of this dream, hitching posts once more began to appear, and with the reappearance of the posts came the rebirth of their tribe, the Buriat nation.

The following day we journeyed to Alhon Island. Alhon Island had been made a world heritage site in 1997. It is a small island, just twenty-two kilometers across. The name Alhon means dry; there is almost no rain in the summer and little snow in the winter. In the old time it was taboo for people other than Shamans to be on the island and women were not allowed on the island until 1970. Lake Baikal, like Lake Aya, has tectonic plates on the bottom of the lake. Perhaps, because of these plates, there is continual, subtle volcanic activity in the lake. To this day the lake is immersed in great mystery.

Just off Alhon Island, on the north side, is a mystical rock called Shaman's Rock. It is actually a rock formed into two peaks connected by a saddle in between. It is one of the world's power points, said to be one of the most Shamanic spots on the planet. I was later told that even in Korea those of Shamanic tradition always turn north to Lake Baikal to honor their distant ancestors. Certainly the energy emanating from this rock was simply amazing! It is said to be inhabited by a special deity called the Great Eagle or Big Bird.

There is a story told about a Shaman who shape-shifted into an eagle so he could fly to Tibet to learn about the Buddhist faith. As the story goes, on the way back the Shaman became hungry and spying a dead horse along the route, stopped to eat it. This action made it then impossible for him to change back to his human form and since that day he has become the mighty Bruhon, a Bourkhan or God, taking the form of an eagle. If you look carefully at pictures of Shaman Rock you will see the image of this mighty eagle emanating from the rock.

Valentin made preparations to hold sacred ceremony. He used milk, saying that the white color was symbolic of purity. New milk was added as each person approached the fire, honoring each person's individual essence. He taught us to extend our arm from the elbow as a sign of respect to the ancestors and deities upon greeting each other.

Our second ceremony was to be a water ceremony down at the lake's edge. It was a ceremony devoted to the waters of Lake Baikal and honored deities, both above and below the waters. Valentin asked us to line up along the water's edge, to the left of him. We were to kneel down on our left knee and, in respect, offer milk to the God of the Lake and all of the princesses. Then we were to wash our elbows, tops of our heads, bottom half of our arms, neck, and face with water from the lake.

Upon completion of the ceremony, Valentin took us down the steep incline to the foot of Shaman's Rock. At the very front of Shaman's Rock was an ancient petroglyph, faintly etched on the rock. It was a magnificent image of Om Mai or the Mother of Us All. It has been there for hundreds of years, no one knows how long.

That evening, after thanking Valentin for sharing his sacred teaching, several of our group wanted to drum around the fire. Soon we were attracting a crowd, many of whom were children. Everyone was curious to see what was happening, seemingly drawn to the rhythm and sound. More and more people began to gather and as they did we looked for things that would help make our percussion orchestra. We had sticks, hinges, saws – anything that would create instruments to accompany the drums. People loved it; the energy was electric and the children were enthralled. The constant drum beat seemed to guide us all back to some beautiful and ancient ritual – back to the place of generations before, embraced in its primal energy. As we continued to play, the sun began to set and vivid color started painting the landscape. Huge splashes of red, orange, and yellow were dappled across the sky, seemingly heightened by the energy we were creating. This magnificent display of color and light started at Shaman's Rock and moved across the sky towards where we were playing, bringing light and joy to us all.

At one point I gave my small drum to one of the very young children. With both passion and focus this tiny little girl began to drum, falling naturally into the rhythm the drum was creating. The look on her little face spoke much more than mere words. Complete happiness and joy for this beautiful young child, who was once more connected to her ancient ways. The drumming became a connection at the deepest level, a true joining of East and West. A connection of sisters and brothers, with gentle blurring of culture or nationality. There was just the drum, the dance, and the circle, the full harmony of people, above, below and all around. True sacred celebration!

Next day I went to explore Shaman's Rock. Each step helped me remember the majesty and wonder of the glorious past of Shamanic tradition. Going back to the times when the Earth was respected and we were Her children and we were still fully connected to Her and Her creatures. I climbed to the saddle between the two peaks. The Om Mai peak on one side and the Great Eagle peak on the other. I sat on a flat outcrop, feeling the balance with the joining of these two peaks – joining of masculine and feminine. Alchemy in nature! Bringing forth a sense of bliss when connected to nature did much toward opening my heart. Mere words cannot describe the moment.

May the journey continue! Ho!

Golden Mountain

The Milky Way that is our path, illuminates our way

Our ancestors walked this path, at times of crossing over

They now extend a helping hand, to help us build tomorrow. M.W.

The Lesson:

A remarkable Elder of heart shares an understanding of the fuller picture.

As my journey continued to take me in search of the old Shamanic wisdom, I would again travel back to the Altai, travelling to the remote village of Mendur Sakkon. Here I would meet Nicholi Shadowev whom I had met the previous summer. This Elder – slight of stature, but big of heart – offered us a huge welcome just as he had the summer before, with fermented mares milk. He was a retired school teacher, writer, and author of many books. He was currently writing about "The Cosmos and Man." As well, he had created a museum in his village and had collected many of his people's legends and stories. He took us now into a yurt-shaped room, where we sat upon benches while he sat on a stool in front – the traditional place when telling stories.

He immediately began to share his wisdom, explaining that there were many clans in his region; he spoke of six clans and six generations. He felt that the old ways of healing were still good and should be used. He also believed it was important to accept all other religions. In 1904, in the village of Kurlic, a new tradition was born. This tradition was called the White Believers. They held their ceremonies only at dawn or during the day. Twice yearly, spring and autumn they held ceremonies. In June, during the new moon they held the green leaf ceremony with prayers for abundance, and then again in autumn, when the leaves turned yellow they asked for protection in the winter months.

Next he described the makeup of humans as he saw it, emphasizing that any living substance has a soul. He felt that when we come back to our pagan roots we begin to understand everything. Every soul has a center in the chest at the moment of conception. Souls are believed to come from the sky and have two charges – positive and negative. They believe that each human has two souls. One soul gives life and the other provides one's karma or fate. Their tradition also teaches that the spirit of death resides near a person. He likened it to the ego in the Western world, and when this spirit becomes out of balance it begins to eat the person (an interesting way to describe an overblown ego).

Nicholi told us that within their tradition they believe that each human is made up of four substances, known as black, white, clear, and wavy, much like the elements, earth, air, water, and fire. These substances determined what kind of person we would be and also who we would interact with. These substances also interact with rays of both the Earth and the sky, hence creating our energy and connection. Energy synchronized from the polar star travels through the sun, the nuclear core of the Earth, and then becomes our source. Nicholi described it being like a huge spiral anchored from the polar star and moving through the sun and the core of the Earth, as an energy coming from source. A huge spiral that was constantly moving and circling all the planets and the stars of our galaxy. It was a movement that spiraled around the Milky Way, much like the movement of lights around a Christmas tree. The entire universe is made up of energy. Each one of us is energy. He stressed that there is energy all around us – everything we touch, see, and feel is alive, each with its own unique form of energy.

He also concluded, while studying the similarities of language between the Altai and the Mayan, that all indigenous peoples of the Earth had a common connection to the Milky Way, but with a slight difference. He said that rather than the Pleiades, as people looked to in the South, the Altai people looked to the North Star. In Altai homes, he explained, there is always an open chimney in honor of the tradition and to remind them of the balance between Earth and sky and the honoring of fire. With this connection we then have the ability to become alive with our inner fire. (1)

In contemplating the wisdom that Nicholi had shared with us, I recalled my own interest in the Milky Way. For some years now there has been a great resurgence of interest in walking the Compostello Trail, known as the trail of the Milky Way. In olden days, pilgrims would make this pilgrimage following the stars overhead in the Milky Way, using it as a kind of compass.

Now only parts of the trail are walked, but in the olden days this pilgrimage started at St Baume, at Mary Magdalene's cave, crossed over the Pyrenees and ended in Finestere, the original location of St James. In Gnostic literature, St James was referred to as the Gate Keeper. Kings, Queens and Heads of State, were compelled to complete this pilgrimage over their lifetimes. They walked from the cave, or the root of the Tree of Life, moving to the final gate or doorway, the crown of the tree. Perhaps they were symbolically walking the path of the Milky Way here on Earth.

In yet even more ancient times we have Machu Pichu in Peru, a huge sacred center that was built as a natural mirror of the Milky Way – again creating the phenomena of as above, so below. In Egypt, Egyptians saw the Nile River as a mirror of the Milky Way, and we can't forget the Pawnee legend that speaks of wolf, The Great Teacher, who travels from Sirius, along the Milky Way, to bring spirit to humans.

How remarkable to realize that this natural phenomena exists also in Russia. This mirror of the Milky Way sits on top of this, their holy mountain, Mount Belukha. From the triple crow of the Great Mother of Us All comes the milky white water of Accem, cascading down into Lake Accem. The lake then feeds into the Accem River and mysteriously disappears into the mountain to reappear and spring forth in the mighty headwaters of the River Katun. This in turn flows across the Altai.

Isn't it remarkable that our ancestors had mapped out the reflection of the Milky Way, creating a natural alchemy of as above, so below? Maybe the message is, and always has been, that the mystery within the Milky Way above can also be mirrored below, here on Earth. As Nicholi reminds us of the honoring of fire in each Altai home, we too can remember that we each possess an inner spark of the divine – our own inner fire.

Edgar Cayce predicted the symbol of the lily as the flower that would symbolize the new Age of Aquarius. It was thought to be symbolic of purity, a bringing of a new time of purity on the planet. Can we hear, touch and smell the fragrance of "spirit knowledge" and step into a new story? Can we do it in time?

As Nicholi brought his presentation to a close, he reminded us the Altai people had suffered greatly throughout their tragic history. He staunchly believed, however, that their land held a special destiny and hoped people would learn to treat his people with kindness and respect. I was touched that Nicholi had been so willing to share his people's traditions and profoundly impressed with his depth of wisdom. In meeting this amazing Elder, I was again impressed by the inherent wisdom and faith of grassroots people, as seen in this amazing Elder with the listening heart.

Sadly we would be leaving the area in the morning, so decided to hold circle in honor of the profound teaching that had been shared with us, and to also honor our Russian sister's birthday. We were staying at a camp near a place called Rosey or White Mountain. Part way up the mountain they had found a large cave containing remnants said to be ancient. There were remains from an ancient fire as well as fragments of pottery. Some felt it dated back to the first people of Altai. A fitting place to hold our honoring ceremony.

I remembered our first circle some years earlier, when I had come to Siberia for the first time, and now in this potent area felt that in some way we were coming full circle. Whereas before we had held a circle in honor of mothers and daughters, this time would be an honoring of grandmothers. We would do a croning for Galina.

In the movement from the mother to the grandmother phase of our lives it is important to acknowledge this new time. This is a stage when our busy time with children has now come to a close and in the old pagan traditions was a time of what they called "the third blood mystery." This meant that we reached menopause, or as they describe it in the old Earth traditions, a time of the "holding of one's blood." It is seen in old traditions as a life cycle when we move into the wisdom years of our lives. Ultimately, it becomes a time to begin to focus more on community and less on hearth. Like the honoring of fire in the Altai, I believe it is important to also reclaim women's transitions. It seemed fitting that we were holding this ceremony on St Mary Magdalene's Day.

We all gathered in one yurt, where earlier we had decorated the space with wildflowers. One of the Canadians had also made a crown of flowers for our honored guest. We had each brought special gifts from Canada and England, in this way paying tribute to our Siberian sister.

We began the ceremony with each of us paying special tribute in words to our dear Siberian sister and ended with the forming of a human birth canal; an initiation where symbolically Galina would have to fight her way out, to a rebirth into her new cycle as wise-woman. As part of our formal ceremony we ended with a gift-giving to Galina. We also presented a drum to her daughter. Spirits were high and Galina looked very beautiful, fully robed in her new role as our newest wise-woman. As I watched each sister paying tribute to their Russian sister, seeing the radiance on each face as we truly shared in the strength that is ours as sisters, I couldn't help surmising that this was indeed the true gold of the Golden Mountain – this legendary mountain. In this moment of honoring the wisdom of one dear sister we had also connected to the place of the Sisters of the Golden Mountain. Here, in this sacred land called the Altai, we had done more than honor a sister. We had also given birth to a sisterhood – to the Sisters of the Golden Mountain.

Next morning, still feeling the warm glow from our sacred circle, Galina said she had a surprise for us. Before leaving Nicholi's area we would drive to the Golden Mountain range. This small range of mountains is said to be very special and there are stories connected to this place about a cave. No one knows for sure where it is, only that it is very deep and holds great mystery. We stopped briefly, taking in the special essence of this golden terrain. Deep essences of mystery, an essence often hidden, yet always there, just like this special connection of sisters. Pure magic; pure gold of the Golden Mountain!

As we began our final journey to the Ust-Koksa region and the village of Chendek, we looked back once more to glimpse the

Golden Mountain, to where its incredible aura, radiating a vibrant golden hue, slowly faded into the landscape.

The journey had given me great gifts, presented in the form of the time honored traditions of the Shamanic ways. The journey also showed me that the Russian people are able to blend the two ways. They connect to the Earth, to their dear Mother Russia, as well as honoring the divine plan of the cosmos, great synthesis of within and without, above and below. I was also cognizant of the gift of meeting remarkable Elders such as Nicholi – an Elder who displayed not only wisdom and integrity, but was also able to express deep love for his country, and to live each day from a place of the listening heart. I am honored and full!

May the journey continue. Ho!

Chapter 17 – Past and Present –
Maria and the Ice Princess

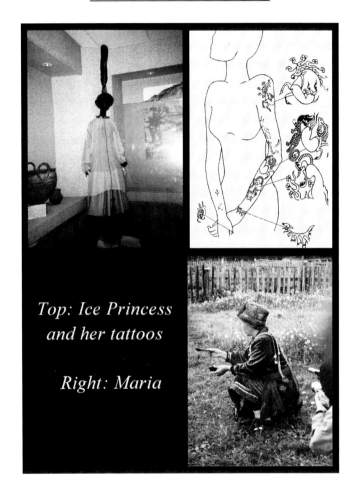

Top: Ice Princess and her tattoos

Right: Maria

"Altai is the navel of the Earth. It belongs not only to us living here, but to all the people of the world." –Maria Amanchina.

Keep this land both clear and bright,
Fulfill the prophecy of the light. M.W.

The Lesson:

Now, with the foundation of the old wisdom in place, the next step of the journey to fire and heart turns to amalgamation – synthesis of past and present.

The people of the Altai have preserved their spiritual roots in spite of a time when religions were silenced. Their spirituality is centered in the belief of Gods and Spirits of Nature. Mountains, rivers, and trees have always been their temples, but in times past, many of the old traditions and ways of practicing spiritual rituals were lost. One of the most powerful revivals is the movement of Akhtyan, proclaiming the white faith of the God Tengri. This following goes back to ancient times to when Altai was the center of the Turkic Kaganat. Shamanism was widely practiced prior to the revolution in 1917, but then became hidden for many years. After Perestroika they were again able to practice more openly. In this setting my journey was now taking me to meet Maria, giving me the gift of synthesis for past and present.

To tell the story of the present day Shaman one must first go back to the distant past. In 1993 Natalia Polishmuk, an archeologist from Novosibirsk, was out in the Ukok Plateau. It was an area that had been considered sacred since ancient times by the people of the Altai. Their beliefs held that the area was part of the heavenly world, the second level of the heavens, nestled in the foothills of the mountain Tabyn-Bodo-Ola. According to legends of old it was also the home of the Scythians, an ancient people of extraordinary abilities.

It was here that this scientist made a huge discovery. Natalia discovered an antiquated crypt that, through a fluke of nature, had mountain water seep into the cavity of the chamber, hence freezing its precious contents. Thus this burial chamber had been preserved for two thousand five hundred years.

Inside the crypt they found the body of a woman, whom they later estimated to be approximately five foot six and somewhere between twenty and thirty years of age. They called her the Ice Princess or Princess of Ukok. It was further determined by the way she had been buried – buried alone, but with six of her horses – as well as the contents of the chamber, that she must have had great status with her people.

Her costume consisted of a silk blouse and skirt, red braided belt, and a three foot tall felt headdress with a mythical griffin depicted at the base. She wore a necklace of wooden camels. All articles had been covered in gold leaf. The princess must have been an imposing figure. She carried a hand mirror – thought to be a sacred object –

and beside her was a small dish containing coriander seeds, possibly used in ritual and prayer.

What was even more mysterious about the frozen princess, however, was that her body was adorned with many tattoos. These tattoos, still clear black markings on her skin, consisted of symbolic drawings of animals, including the mythical griffin both on her thumb and again on her left arm. Scientists concluded that the tattoos were marks of a spiritual leader. The griffin, dating back to ancient times, often symbolized great gifts including shape-shifting and were frequently talismans for Healers and Shamans. The turkey vulture is thought to be a descendent of the griffin. To ancient Assyrians the griffin was the guardian of life, death, and transformation. (1)

Who was the Ice Princess? Perhaps a Shaman, a Healer, or a revered storyteller. She was buried in a coffin sculpted from a single larch tree. The larch tree has long been considered sacred to local people. It is often symbolic of the Tree of Life, so death becomes a returning to the Tree of Life.

Controversy rages over the location for the final resting place of the Ukok Princess. Scientists want to continue their study and research, whereas the Altai people see the bigger picture from a spiritual perspective and want the Princess returned home. They believe that by moving her, she and the area have been desecrated.

Over the ensuing years of debate several people have become connected to the Ice Princess in a special way. One in particular is an

Altai Shaman called Maria. Maria comes from the Koshagach region of Altai and she belongs to the Telyos Syok tribe, her ancestors originating from the Lake Teletskoe region. Nowadays she lives in Ust Khan.

Maria is a petite woman with prominent Mongolian features and displays a beautiful dimpled smile. Her call to the Shaman's path came early. Typically, she didn't really want to become a Shaman, but finally accepted destiny as the alternative would have been becoming ill, or worse – to die.

The sacred totem for her tribe is the hare. When still quite young, she was told to look inside an old family chest belonging to her grandmother for a hare skin. To her surprise, when she went to look, the hare skin was there. Since then, Maria keeps this talisman in a special bag, complete with the picture of a hare on the outside, and hangs it on the wall of her ail (yurt).

When we arrived in Maria's village we were immediately taken to her ail. Inside, a fire burns in the middle of it. Maria's sacred bundles hang on the far wall of the yurt. It is customary on entering a yurt to pay your respect by bowing to the fire.

Maria kindly agreed to describe some of the traditions that her tribe observes. She told me that unlike our traditions in North America, they don't honor the elementals as such, with the exception of fire, but rather they believe that every field, every creek and mountain has its own spirits. The mountain passes are considered powerful and it is suggested that while travelling through passes one should cover the head to show respect. Often prayer ties are offered when making prayers. Two pieces of cloth are used, usually white, and are tied on a branch of a shrub or tree, tied with the knot upward and facing east.

Their tradition in the Altai is to honor the corners of Altai rather than the Four Directions. When communicating with spirit (their helpers or guardians) they do their ceremonies in sets of three. For example, when calling to their helpers they would bow three times, each time offering milk or vodka. Prayers too are always repeated three times over. If making a presentation to a respected visitor they would present three yards of white cloth. This ceremony was done after I had given Maria a drum. She in return had presented me with three yards of white cloth.

Maria feels it is her role to revive their traditional ceremonies – a great responsibility that she carries for her people. She also has another important mission; along with eight other people on the planet, she holds a special connection to the Ice Princess. Her greatest hope is that the Ice Princess will be returned to the Altai. In communication with the Ice Princess, Maria has been told we must all begin to respect Mother Earth, and with the Altai having the distinction of being the navel of the planet, she feels that it is vital that the beautiful Ice Princess be returned home. This would help balance present with the past.

With the removal of the Ice Princess, the workers began to have terrifying nightmares. There were unexplained deaths and some people who lived nearby lost all their hair. The sacred site appears to have been disturbed and the area appears to have become unbalanced. Since having spoken with my friend, a Shaman of the Romany tradition, she has told me of the dangers of releasing energies known as the "black waters." That is, when a sacred site is excavated often very negative energy is released which may cause havoc.

In an attempt to bring about more balance, Maria has received permission from the Museum to sit with the Ice Princess and to work in bringing the soul of the Princess back to the Altai. In her heart, Maria hopes the body will also be returned.

I was able to visit the Ice Princess, truly a great honor. Scientists have indeed learned much from this amazing discovery. Each time I go back to pay my respects to this amazing ancestor of our distant past, it is quite obvious that she is slowly deteriorating. Perhaps the time has come for the Princess to be honored by giving her the rest she so richly deserves in her native land.

The Altai is an amazing place with unique and powerful energies. It is a true amalgamation of past and present. It also holds a great destiny for our whole planet, but cannot do it alone. We must give our special ancestors like the Ice Princess and Shamans like Maria our respect and support, especially given that the Altai is a special place on the planet that still carries uninterrupted, continuous homage to Mother Earth. This surely contributes highly to a balance sorely needed in today's world.

With the synthesis of past and present this segment of my journey was complete. May the journey continue. Ho!

Chapter 18 – Miracle of the Red Rose

Mary and the red rose

"A new dawn for mankind will come when the understanding of Fire enters life." (1)

What is the mystery, held dear in the rose?
What is it that captures both my heart and my soul? M.W.

The Lesson:

Preparation for the fiery experience was made through a deeper connection to land and wisdom. In creating "fiery baptism," one must experience the opening of the heart center or opening of the fifth petal. In this new rhythm, fire of the heart is said to unite through its magnet with a remarkable consequence of regeneration. Fire is the hearth of transmutation. (2)

Our small group of heroines of the East-West connection was at it again. We decided once again to put on another family camp. We were calling it "Entering the Circle," but more specifically we hoped to focus on what we thought of as creating the new story – very simply, a new story for a new time, to try and live in that sacred place of beauty. We also wished to explore the concept of destiny. This new act of power was to push us into the third initiation into fire.

Since heroine acts are essentially "fiery deeds," we were reminded by Agni Yoga to nourish this feat with joy, courage, and endurance, steadfastly overcoming each obstacle as it was presented. It had been two years since our last camp so much anticipation, joy, and excitement were easily maintained.

Agni Yoga teaches that fire is the highest element – the only element that brings higher consciousness. Fire can be described as the most all-pervading, creative, and most life bearing of all the elements (3). Just as the elements with lightning had intensified our inner fires in our first camp, and the mask in the second camp, we now hoped to manifest a similar experience in our search for the new story.

Soon camp preparations were underway. Camp would be held in a different location, but still by the Sylva River. Setting up the world altar, we also decided to hold morning ceremonies as we had in the other two camps. This included calling out the Four Directions and smudging, as well as closing with Eastern mantras. This would provide a basis for our East-West synthesis. I planned to work on destiny material, or exploration of our new paths, so began working with guided Shamanic journeying to this end. Each participant would make a shield that would depict how they visualized their life path. With the children it would be altered slightly. Younger people would make a shield that would describe how they could be heroes, much like the folktales of the Firebird. In the Agni Yoga teachings this was described as an act of povod or courage. People came with many different expectations of camp, but mostly, however, they felt it was now a different time and they were searching as to how best to proceed. Many put it simply as learning to help their families and others to live in a better way.

Some time before coming to camp I'd had another Shamanic dream. In the dream I saw an exotic looking man approaching me dressed in an old fashioned tuxedo complete with swallow tails. On his left lapel he wore a gilded calla lily. Aside from being curious about the lily, I was also drawn to this man's eyes. Eyes are the conduit of fiery energy (4). They appeared as deep dark pools of wisdom and I knew that I was gazing into the eyes of my Master. With that, I woke up, knowing I had to research the meaning of the lily.

The lily is a universal symbol portraying magnificent beauty, perfection, and truth. A symbol that helps us unite our world of diversity. In Islamic tradition it is called Iah – the flame of unity, light, and consciousness. In Christianity it is the Easter lily. The Masters are said to wear garments which display a flame in the shape of a calla lily over their heart center. This flame symbolically represents the flame of truth. The inexplicable scent of either a lily or rose indicates the presence of a Master.

As I researched the symbol of the lily, universal to all faiths, I became intrigued by a reading by Edgar Cayce. He had spoken of the lily, its meaning I had spoken of earlier as being the symbol for the new epoch. It was stated as follows:

Q .13 "Is the Aquarian age described as the 'age of the Lily,' and why?"
A .13 "The purity. Only the purity as it represents will be able to comprehend or understand that awareness that is before those who seek the way." (Edgar Cayce Reading #1602-3.) (5)

The Agni Yoga teachings stress that to be initiated into the realm of fire one must achieve a level of purity – not only in the physical, but also in our consciousness as well (6). Approaching with an open heart was vital, only then are we able to see real beauty. It was this purity of body, mind, and soul that we strived to work towards in this third camp. Good food, banya (Russian steam bath) ceremonies, prayer, and meditation, as well as movement, dance, and Qigong, all contributed in their unique ways.

I'd had banya before, but at this camp it was extremely well set up. There were three rooms – one for changing clothes, one for washing and rinsing, and the third was where the actual steam was. The steam room contained a stove in the middle with hot rocks on top, where one could add water to create the steam. The stove was surrounded by tiered wooden planks where you could sit or lie to get the full benefit of the steam. There were bundles of birch leaves tied together, used to beat your skin to increase your circulation.

I was quite shocked the first time my dear Russian sisters helped me with my steam bath. They said briefly in English, "Now we will beat you." I didn't know what to expect and prepared for some strange Russian initiation. They dipped the birch bundle into hot water and by shaking this over my body, created the moisture needed for the next step. Then they began slapping my body all over with birch leaves, which leaves a residue of oil on your skin to nourish it. When finished, the body feels glowing and exhilarated. Next was the massage, followed by the final stage: going into the second room for further scrubbing with loofah sponges to wash the body. One emerges not only feeling squeaky clean, but also nurtured and nourished.

Over the following days we worked with a process called "soul retrieval." This is a unique healing process that one does in

163

Shamanic tradition after an individual experiences loss of bits of their soul. This can happen after surgery, for example, or when a woman goes into shock after giving birth, or it could be some trauma like a car accident. There are many ways this can happen and then the person begins to experience a loss in their vital life energy. A Shaman skilled in these methods can then go through a process of retrieval, usually aided by a drum. It is a very complex form of healing. In a group setting, however, we worked through guided visualization or journeying. We also utilized ecstatic healing trance and special dance movements, as well as Qigong each morning. This prepared participants, as they began making their shields, to depict their new story as they saw it.

Morning dawned with mist rising off the river. Outside my tiny cabin was a tree with no less than seven perfect spider's webs shining and crystallized by the mist. It promised to be a beautiful day. As we began our morning workshop a family arrived. They had gone back to Perm overnight and now came into the workshop and presented me with a huge, perfect, deep red rose, freshly picked from their garden. They told me it was in honor of the guided meditations we had been doing, but for me it went much deeper. This red rose was a symbol of Mary Magdalene, so this touching gift was deeply profound. I instantly felt a faint flutter in my chest and instinctively knew I had opened my heart. Simultaneously, I sensed a subtle tremor throughout my body, somewhat like a pulse, as heat surged through my entire body. Coupled with the tremor and heat came clarity of thought, often described as second thought or second sight. It was the intensifying of psychic energy (7). Generally our energy operates from our solar plexus and the other centers below the waist. This could be over lifetimes. When our heart center opens, a new rhythm is established and we are then able to access the centers above the heart. This instigates a refinement of energy. Psychic energy can then be heightened, thus helping us see in an enhanced way; Agni Yoga suggests that this rarely happens without a prolonged period of being immersed in nature. Though I would not grasp the full spectrum of the shift until later, there was also a much deeper and profound shift that placed us in a finely tuned balance with spirit. Now, suddenly we were open to a delicate collaboration with spirit.

In the book *Serving Humanity* by Alice Bailey, it is said: *"When the hour has come,"* (and already a few cases are to be found) *"many cases of overshadowing will be seen and will demonstrate in a threefold manner."* (8)

The book goes on to explain that there is "an over shadowing of one's work by the 'great Ones' and can only happen when the fifth petal – that is the heart – is open." (9)

Agni Yoga tells us that fire transforms all fiery substances and reveals the luminous matter found in everything that exists (10). The fiery heart does this also. As I looked now around our group, glowing faces looked back. It was as though we had all been bathed in pure liquid light. We were again in fire's workshop. In a sense, camp became an experiment in loving community, co-creating with spirit. So just like the first camp with the lightning, now with the opening of the fifth petal, heat blossomed all around us, bringing tender healing to us all.

Now camp was the same, but different – our vibratory energy had changed. Suddenly the need to solve problems wasn't so important because people began to feel filled, more in balance with nature and able to focus on beauty. I had gone out to visit the ruins of an old monastery with the family who had brought me the rose and while I was away the Russians totally transformed the camp. Flowers and herbs were now ensconced everywhere, including inside the outhouses. A soft, warm glow permeated everything.

One woman said she had witnessed a globe of light the night before up in the sky. This globe of light moved closer and hung over the camp. In the morning it was still there. Our small camp was approaching the fine tuned balance of one with spirit and it was remarkable!

Groups took on a different tone, moving into a place of celebration. We held a mother-daughter celebration. Everyone was dressed in crowns of flowers. One of the common comments from women at the beginning of camp was that they wanted to feel more "womanly," and we were now celebrating ourselves as women. We needed to begin to remember who we were as women, especially our passion and our beauty.

"It is necessary to awaken in woman herself a great respect for her own Origin: she should realize her great destiny as a bearer of higher energy." (11)

Part of the celebration was to invite young women into womanhood and to this end we had the young women line up at one end with the older women, the mothers, forming a tunnel through which the young women had to pass. Just as in real life, the older women would mimic difficult life passages and not make it easy for the younger ones to get through. In forming this human labyrinth, the older women, with the aid of the hand drum, encouraged each young woman to come through. Each young maiden pushed herself through the barrier of the maze. With extreme effort each young women made it through to womanhood on the other side. It was great fun! All reported being successful in feeling womanly, feeling beautiful and feeling alive! In acting out this transition at a physical level it felt more real, becoming an integrated experience.

During the course of camp several of us had visits from the mouse. In my Shamanic tradition it is always important to note the animals that appear, especially at times of ceremony or transition. Animals or birds enhance the clues set out for one's journey. When I had done the guided journey for the children, to find their power animal, two or three of the young children had seen mice. Also, when individuals had done their ceremonies for their shield, they had experiences with mice. One young man, for example, had left his prayer beads on top of his shield over night. He went back to retrieve the shield in the morning, only to discover that the mice, overnight, had eaten the string of the prayer beads right through in several places. I too had ended up having a mouse running around in my room, much to the consternation of both the mouse and myself. The mouse, in my tradition, comes from the South direction on the medicine wheel. It is said to be about looking close up through the eyes of an innocent – to see things close up from a place of total innocence, just like a child.

We also had several who had experiences with the hawk – a bird that always seems present when I am in Russia. The family that had given me the rose had even found a dead hawk and given me several of the bird's feathers. This animal is connected to the East of the medicine wheel and is what I call one of the ancient messengers. Like the eagle, they see the furthest and fly the highest, taking our prayers to spirit. What a potent combination – to walk in trust and innocence with mouse, while being able to fly high and connect to spirit with our messenger hawk. Blend of spirit and matter couched within fire's workshop.

Our fiery experience would also have a profound affect on the children. After the second camp, one of the girls decided she must go and see Sri Baba. She spent the next year planning to do this and set off for India on her own, succeeding with her plan. She was only fourteen at the time. Another girl had begun to paint and to read very deep esoteric books. One day I went into the workshop area to find a young boy there, sitting in front of the altar, deep in prayer.

The one that mystified me the most was a young boy who had attended all three camps with his parents. He was intrigued by the ceremony we did each morning, especially when we smudged with sage. During all the camps he was most particular that he be smudged only by me. Outside of circle he appeared to be just an ordinary boy, but once in circle he seemed to turn into this old Master. By the end of camp he was teaching several of the other little boys how to be in circle. He was seven. I have since been told that once he got home he took the sage stick that I had given him as a gift and set up his own altar, without any assistance from his parents. True wisdom in the heart of innocence!

Agni Yoga emphasized moving from a place of only knowledge, to the softer realm of sensing, similar to the ways of the Shamanic tradition. Thought combined with fire becomes creative thought – a heightened human experience. The teachings tell us that clairvoyance and clairaudience are really fire-voyance and fire-audience. In other words, enhanced or heightened psychic energy. (12)

Sadly, camp was coming to a close. Camp had exceeded anything any of us had experienced before. Fire can be best manifested through color and sound. As a closing, everyone participated in an ecstatic trance posture called "The Singing Shaman," a posture used for celebration (13). We assumed the posture and began the trance with the sound "ahh." As the trance progressed, each participant was taken down their own path into harmonics. The exquisite sound that rose up from all of the participants was incredible. There are simply no words to describe the energy being projected through our sound. An amazing ending to an amazing camp!

The red rose is a symbol for Mary Magdalene. This beautiful flower had unfurled our hearts, bringing us a brief glimpse of what true community, created by fiery achievement, really could be when we walked with spirit. Through innocence and an open heart it gave us a taste of how we could live our new story if we chose to come alive with fire and walk with spirit.

With gratitude and love to my beloved ones, may the journey continue. Ho!

Chapter 19 – Travelling to Eden

Left: Journey to Mylobka   Right: Snake Mountain

May we drink of new purity, taken in sips

Wisdom of Mother, once more on our lips. M.W.

The Lesson:

After initiation into the fiery experience, expressing gratitude becomes an integral part of the journey. Gratitude can be expressed through celebration in nature.

171

I have often felt that an experience of true celebration rests in our connection with nature. When I step out into the primitive world of nature and see the shading of greens dappled by sunlight and the drops of rain left on each tender leaf, forming crystal prisms of light, that mysterious excitement of the unknown begins. Stepping fully into the experience, a hush falls over this magnificently painted landscape, exuding a stillness that penetrates to one's very soul. Yet within this mystical stillness is a tender quickening, a kind of excitement that has no name. As it takes shape and begins to surface one can sense around the edges of this exquisite moment the true meaning of reverence – the childlike wonder one feels when we see the full panoramic grandeur before us. In true celebration we become truly alive!

This kind of celebration came in the form of a surprise from the camp organizers. Rather than experiencing a dreaded backlash from the profound experience we'd had at camp, we would move instead into celebration. I had heard of a mysterious place called "the zone" for some years now and this was where they were taking me. When I asked about its location and size everything was a mystery. They said the zone is constantly moving and changing so no one really knows its size. The only thing they know is that for some reason this place is more active in the fall, but they don't know why.

I had been trying to get into this mystical place since 1999. In the early nineties my friend Carol, from England, had been taken into the zone further north and during her visit had gone swimming. She sensed the place being full of light and later discovered, upon developing her photos, that distinct balls of light were suspended over the water where she swam. I was excited at the prospect of experiencing this mysterious place first hand. As well, going into power spots such as the zone helps to integrate deep experiences such as the fiery experience we had encountered at camp.

In the early eighties a man travelled to the Perm region. He started an Agni Yoga group, also working with the devotees of Krishna. They stumbled upon a place where the energy seemed very potent and alive. This was the zone. They described it as being a place so alive, it seemed as if the air around them was breathing. The group believed that this place had in ancient times been home to the Rishis. They felt, too, that it was a powerful place of healing.

With camp ending we set off to the small village of Mylobka, situated by the Mylobka River, just on the edge of the zone. Mylobka means literally "the place of prayer," and this small village was said to date back to ancient times as a place of worship. In the late 1800s there was a large copper plant here and the village was much bigger. At the time of the revolution the family who owned the copper plant left the region and there has been no mining in the region since. The village now seems all but forgotten.

Archeological research has determined through the discovery of bones from different sites that the Mansi tribe once lived there. For this tribe, the Gods of the elements played an important part in their spiritual life and bear was a vital symbol of this belief (the bear later became the symbol of Perm). There was, at one time, three tribes situated in the region, but the Mansi tribe was the oldest of these. The reverence for nature in the region was hence very strong and continuous since ancient times, which some of the local people estimate to be as far back as 4000 BC.

Mylobka eventually became Christianized and churches were built on the old tribal stone altars. It then went through a period of history when it was predominantly a Christian center. The village today is smaller and, like many villages, poor but self-sufficient.

All of us were weary after camp and looked forward to an early night, given that we would be getting up very early to make our way into the zone. Mysteriously, a white dog appeared – a scruffy lookalike to my beloved companion back home. She chose to sleep beside my bed during the night. Sometime during the night I woke up suddenly; I sat up and glanced over to the window in the room. It was completely dark now in the tiny village, but through the window I could see four large globes of white light, and they appeared suspended and framed in the window. They seemed to be in a square formation, with two at the top and two at the bottom. As I watched this unusual light phenomenon the globes began to flick off and on, as if attached to a light switch. The light pattern followed a

174

deliberate clockwise sequencing. This strange harmonics of light continued for some time. It made me think of the camp and how we had honored the Four Directions each morning in camp as a part of our opening ceremony. I was intrigued by this same clockwise sequencing from the cosmos.

Reluctantly I got up and went out to the back yard to the outhouse. There I saw a single globe of light also suspended in the night sky. This single globe was soft orange in color. By now I was fully awake, aware that this wasn't just a dream. I went back to bed and continued to watch the four globes in the sky displayed fully in the bedroom window across from my bed. Finally I was too tired to watch any longer and drifted off to sleep, fully anticipating the promise of new adventure in the morning.

It was now very early morning. Hasty preparations were made for breakfast and the beginning of this special journey into the zone. Our party of fourteen made our way down to the river's edge. There we would be meeting our guide Nicholas and my special mode of transportation. Nicholas was already there when we arrived. He was a local villager who had hunted many years in the zone and knew it well. He was a handsome man in his sixties with silver hair and striking eyes. He warned the group to be vigilant as they walked, as there were many snakes in the area and all were poisonous.

Next the driver arrived. He drove up, standing in a small cart being pulled by a silvery white horse. He was to drive the cart into the zone. My transportation for the day's journey had just appeared! Nicholas, Emil (the driver), and I, along with everyone's gear, were to travel in this small two-wheeled cart. The rest of my courageous Russian friends were going to walk ten kilometers into the zone, have lunch and hold a circle, and then walk the ten kilometers back out. My admiration for my brave companions soared!

Now plans began to be made to cross the river. I was becoming very apprehensive. Soon it was my turn to get in the cart and make my way across. The valiant horse made her way slowly, straining and slipping on the wet rocks. The water steadily climbed higher and higher around our vehicle. I held on in pure terror, clutching frantically to the sides of the cart as we bounced over the river rock bed. Soon, however, levels began to drop and we were approaching the river's edge on the other side. The first obstacle had been overcome.

Into the zone we now went, winding our way through dense undergrowth and forest. Soon we came to a slight rise and our guide informed us that we were now officially entering the zone. Our group went over to a nearby birch tree and tied a white prayer tie on one of the branches, thanking through prayer the ancestors and spirits of place for the incredible privilege of being there. We slowly made our way deeper into this amazing force of nature, an area untouched by human influence. As I hung on – bouncing, jolting, and shaking my way into the zone – I was transfixed by what surrounded me. Flowers and herbs made up the floor of the forest.

Colors of every description were displayed on the magical, green undergrowth. Pinks, lavenders, yellows, oranges, and blues splotched the green carpet and clearly fed one's soul. Some of the flowers were similar to plants I had seen in other regions.

What was truly spectacular, however, was that instead of being waist high or lower, the plants here towered over us in heights up to five feet and more. Never had I witness such a glorious profusion of growth. It felt as if I had somehow wandered into some magical fairy realm – which indeed I had. The atmosphere of this whole place was alive and breathing! With each breath our souls were being filled to overflowing with the divine beauty of nature as guides, horse, cart, and I broke trail, with my staunch Russian friends following closely behind. It was getting warm now and the flies had come out to join us. With the constant jostling of the cart we were in constant and perpetual motion. At times we had to negotiate fallen trees, looking for alternative ways around; then, at other times, we would hit the huge ruts hidden in the high grass and careen off to one side as one wheel would suddenly drop into a huge hole, with me wondering if I would be catapulted out of the cart entirely. I worked continuously at just hanging on. By now each cell in my body had been shaken, bent, and reassembled in a whole new order.

As my whole body screamed, aching from the constant jolts and movements, we moved into a clearing. We had made the ten kilometers and had now arrived at Silva River, close to the confluence of Silva and the Mylobka rivers. Moving into the clearing fully, the area gave way to an expanse of space where the flowing Silva wove her way through the rocks and trees. It was beautiful. On either side of the river were cliffs, looking like two arms jutting out in prominence. Someone said that the Ancients felt that at one time these two arms had been joined. Now what remained was the space where the river flowed serenely through, appearing to create a mystical doorway into the unknown. On our side of the river was Snake Mountain. We had arrived at our destination.

While others began preparations for lunch, I went over to get a closer look at the rock formations. The rocks were light ginger in color and looked extremely ancient. Much of the rock appeared layered and looked almost man-made, somewhat like stacked pieces of a huge pyramid. It was most unusual. I asked Nicholas and the driver if they would stand at the base of Snake Mountain so I could take their picture. Having agreed to this, I pushed the button on my camera. Nothing happened. I tried again – still nothing. Finally, on the last try the camera lurched into motion and I took the shot. It was not unusual in this area to find cameras would not work, perhaps because of the high mineral content.

One of the camp organizers had written me earlier about Snake Mountain. A group of them had gone into the zone and got lost. Just as they were beginning to worry, a man appeared out of nowhere. He guided them to Snake Mountain and then prepared to leave. The group felt a sense of panic and said, "But how will we find our way back out?" He told them not to worry, that as long as they had their drum they would be fine.

Over lunch I asked people to share some of the experiences they'd had in the zone. Nicolas began with a story about a particular day he went hunting. As he was returning home he walked through a meadow and suddenly heard a loud noise. It was like a large animal walking in the forest and he imagined he could even hear it breathing. He was very afraid, so he shot his gun into the air to try to warn off whatever might be following him. He walked quickly, finally arriving home without mishap. Next morning, he went out to check and found the footprints of a wild boar. In speaking to neighbors of the incident, it was reported by several that they had seen a bright light coming from the area in which he had heard this strange noise. He said one particular area, said to be where a UFO landed, always fills him with fear despite the fact that he has hunted around it all his life. The locals tell a story of natives of the area sighting a UFO, after which the cattle were afraid and wouldn't graze there.

They spoke also of the many times people would come to make a documentary of the area, only to discover their camera equipment didn't work and some even felt they were being watched. One lady described camping one time by the river, and there was a thunderstorm. During the storm, when she closed her eyes she saw appear before her vision an ongoing stream of symbols. Although not familiar to her, she sensed the symbols of letters and numbers were ancient. Three years later she was again camping with her family very near the zone. A huge storm erupted and they went and hid in the tent. Huge trees began to fall and a boat flew by just thirty meters from their tent. Great strips of forest were uprooted and houses in the village were damaged. In the short space of thirty minutes, while the storm continued to rage around them, she said she continued to pray. When it was over they were unhurt. This violent storm took place only in this small area and she felt it had been nature's way of cleansing the place.

With stories and lunch over, we decided it was time to hold the circle on top of Snake Mountain. Each person would bring a stone with them up the mountain so they could begin building a medicine wheel. They could add to it each time they came back to the area. We lined the circle up with an old fire pit that looked out onto the river. This created a full alignment with the two rock arms on each side of the river. We would honor this mystical doorway. As we gathered together in the circle on top of the mountain, I called out to the ancestors, to the Four Directions, and to our guides and spirits of this place with the drum. I also honored the Lords of Nature who seemed to rule supreme here. The sound coming from the drum was deep, resonant, and clear. The energy in the circle was palpable as each individual put out their prayers in their own way, asking for blessings for themselves, the circle, and this truly beautiful place. This was the first time that the guides had participated in circle like this and they appeared deeply touched. We could all feel the oneness – a deep heart connection once more to community and nature.

As we began our trek back, with me once again jostling along in the cart, I recalled the conversation we had had over lunch. I had asked very simply, "Why is this place so special?" The Russians said that there were many, many minerals here and just maybe that is what creates the special energy. They went on to describe how in prehistoric times the mountains here had been quite high, but with the ice age things had shifted and moved and many minerals had come to the surface. Whatever the reasons, the radium emissions here were unusually high and the electro-magnetic energy is very strong; certainly the strongest I had ever experienced.

There is a legend about this place that at one time a piece of the bright star Venus broke off and landed in the forest here. The sun came along one day and spotted this broken part of Venus and assisted its return back home. Since then, energy remains potent, nature continues to rule undisturbed, and in so doing attracts the cosmic rays which maintain the energy (1). As above, so below! Regardless of the reason, I came away grateful that I had been privileged to go into the zone, to this small patch of Eden – going to a place where Mother Earth was still very much alive, protected, and honored. I am thankful and I am full!

Let the journey continue. Ho!

Chapter 20 – Coming Full Circle

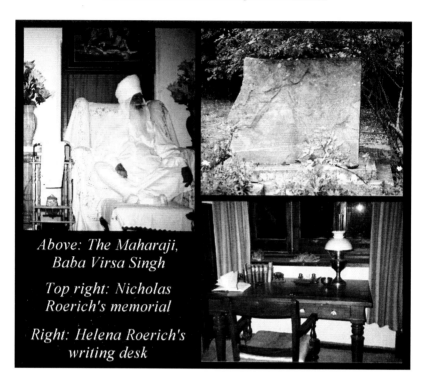

*Above: The Maharaji,
Baba Virsa Singh*

*Top right: Nicholas
Roerich's memorial*

*Right: Helena Roerich's
writing desk*

Each step a journey, each journey a step

The Holy footprint comes into view. M.W.

The Lesson:

Fire is never constant; it is perpetually in the process of evolution or involution. The student, to keep the embers alive, must ever push forward, striving towards goals and ultimately larger destinies. The engine for this is passion.

The journey within Shamanic tradition always follows the great round. That is, the student or pilgrim travels in a circle. The journey had provided many lessons, from sacred connection to the land and the many teachings of Shamanic traditions to the bold workshops into fire. My sense was, however, that I was now beginning to move full circle. The journey began with the introduction to Agni Yoga and now, coming full circle, I would travel to the Roerich estate in India. What were these new teaching now about to be revealed?

Fire, unlike other elements, doesn't come from something – it must be manifested. Ironically, although constant in its nature, fire is not static; rather the element of fire is constantly in the process of evolution/involution (1). Fire must continually be fuelled to stay alive so in a journey one maintains a forward movement, striving always to new goals. Joeseph Campbell described this quite succinctly by saying, "Always follow your bliss."(2) Quite simply, when we follow our passion, passion follows us. When we keep the embers of fire alive, goals become acts and acts ultimately push us forward towards specific paths of destiny.

Throughout the journey I had been drawn to the work of Nicholas and Helena Roerich. The teachings of Agni Yoga had provided a profound foundation and understanding for our fiery experience at the last camp. Two other aspects of their work also rendered a huge impact on the journey – one being unity of women and the second the special destiny of Russia. Churchill once described Russia as "a riddle wrapped in a mystery inside an enigma." As my journey shifted towards full circle this enigma held great intrigue.

Galina had invited me to an international forum for peace, to be hosted by a community called Gobind Sadan, just outside Delhi. The Guru of Gobind Sadan, Baba Virsa Singh, held special insights about Russia. I hoped to meet him so I could learn more.

In the mid 1920s, the Masters had asked the Roerichs to carry the Mahatma's Message to Moscow. The couple also brought a small ivory casket containing soil sanctified by Buddha as a gift. The Masters wished to encourage those searching for community or brotherhood. They also wanted the Altai recognized as a special spiritual place, hoping to build a temple there.

The message was not well received and the Roerichs fled for their life, ending up in the tiny village of Uimon in Siberia. They stayed in the village prior to their Altai-Himalaya journey. After this journey they settled instead in Kulla Valley where they founded the Research Institute Urusvati. Urusvati, meaning Morning Star, was an institute of learning and research for science, arts, and religion. It was at Urusvati Estate in Naggar, Kulla Valley that Nicholas Roerich spent the remaining years of his life.

After the conference, a small group of delegates from the conference made our way into the Himalayas and Kulla Valley. As we moved into the mountains my excitement soared. I had read so much about these mystical mountains, including the many legends of Shambhala. Going to the Roerich estate was now pushing the journey forward.

Kulla Valley is home of many ancient kings. It is protected by three hundred and sixty Gods and it was a famous ancient trade route to Ladakh and Tibet. Even Alexander the Great is said to have reached Kulla Valley. The Roerich Estate is located outside the small village of Naggar.

Upon arriving in Naggar we made our way to the Roerich estate. Outside the Roerich house was a collection of statues of Gods and Goddesses which had been collected by the Roerichs; the central one, being female, was called Guga Chokhan. A local priest did ceremony twice daily in honor of them. He was a descendent of the priest that had done ceremony when Nicholas and Helena lived there. His ceremony was very powerful and I was touched by the deep reverence with which the priest paid honor to the Gods and the Goddesses.

The next morning I took a walk along a path that meandered down to the lower levels of the estate. I arrived at an enclosure where a very large stone had been erected. It was the memorial to Nicholas Roerich, the place where his ashes rested. After paying quiet tribute to this great Master, I went to the back of the enclosure to sit on a bench there. I was immediately surrounded by a deeply peaceful energy. The vista of the entire valley lay before my gaze, including the two white peaks that formed a perfect M and which had been dubbed Morya's Mountain by the Roerichs. The vision was breathtaking! I could imagine the Roerichs spending time here in quiet meditation, surrounded by this natural beauty.

That evening the curator took me to see Helena's writing room. Here was the place, considered by some, which the highest spiritual teachings had been written and which were now distributed throughout the world. I felt so honored that this had been a part of my journey. Amidst the distinct smell of roses, the presence of Helena felt very near and I knew I had indeed come full circle.

Nicholas and Helena worked tirelessly, Nicholas with painting, research and writing and Helena with her writing. Although they would never return to their beloved Russia, they continued to believe in the special destiny of their homeland. Consistent reference was made to the New Country or Northern Shambalha, always alluding to Russia's special role.

They were not alone in this prophecy. As you may recall, I described how Edgar Cayce, the sleeping prophet, reiterated this vision in 1932, 1938, and again in 1944.

"In Russia there comes the hope of the world, not as that sometimes termed of Communistic, or Bolshevistic, no. But freedom, freedom!

That each man will live for his fellow man!" (Edgar Cayce Reading #3976-29.) (3)

This prophecy was also widely written of by Alice Bailey from 1919 to 1949 when she spoke of a New World religion destined to unfold in the Aquarian Age. In her book, *The Destiny of Nations*, she refers to Russia as a place that out of its unique mystical quality will emerge the ability to link the East and the West (4). Rudolph Steiner and, more recently, Sun Bear reiterated this same prophecy. Sun Bear stating: *"I do see an awakening in some parts of Russia to their old Shamanic knowledge. This will eventually result in the prophetic knowledge coming out of Russia to other parts of the planet."* (5)

As well, Baba Virsa Singh also spoke of visions he has had concerning Russia's special role "should they choose to take this path." It was time now to return to the community to see if I could gain audience with him to hear his thoughts on this first hand.

His story had always intrigued me because since childhood he had spoken of Russia as having a special destiny. I was hoping he would speak of this. Gobind Sadan was founded in 1968, when Babaji transformed a rocky jungle into a flourishing farm. Since that time he has also taken barren land along the Ganges River, which had once been subjected to constant flooding, and turned it into a successful operation, making the mission fully self-supporting. The farm is called Shiv Sadan (house of Shiva). Each year his followers have steadily increased, including many, many Russians that make

187

pilgrimage to the community. From the time of his childhood visions, Baba Virsa Singh was shown a future where Russia was destined to have a very special role. He stated very clearly that, *"There is no doubt that when these waves arise in Russia they will spread throughout the world. You have said 'No God' for a long time. Now you will say, 'One God.'"* Baba Virsa Singh honored all great teachers believing in the oneness of all beings and all religions under "One God." (6)

Maharaj first visited Russia in 1989 and he warned that the Soviet Union would fall apart if economic reforms were pushed too fast. He promised to return when Russia was ready to recognize its true mission. The Maharaj and Russia seem linked in a unique and intricate way. I was most anxious to hear his thoughts. It was late evening when Galina got word that the Maharaj would see our group. After our initial greetings, Galina had an opportunity to ask about Russia's special destiny.

His Holiness first explained that Russians have had a very long history of suffering, so are able to understand other peoples, other nations. Then he said very simply: *"Russians have very clean hearts – they have not bothered to separate heart from head. With pure hearts, Russians can and do connect deeply to spirit – to God."* (7)

What a wonderful affirmation! My experience throughout my travels in Russia had been just as the Maharaj had described – true heart connection to all whom I would meet. This vast and wondrous country had held a secret, one that had been dormant and hidden from the Western world for so many years. Perhaps now was the time to celebrate this special destiny and share it with the rest of the world. I truly hope so.

I had come full circle. My journey to Russia carried such a simple message – to return to heart, return to the sacred, while always remembering Mother Earth, and to always keep the fire within alive. A Russian historian, Gumilev, spoke of people with a passionate heart. He called them "passionariy." Moving now to the final curtain of the journey, may we step into the role of passionariy, becoming those new pilgrims who have bold, listening hearts.

May the journey continue. Ho!

Top: Croning in honor of the grandmothers
Left: Wild woman, Queen of the Forest
Right: Youngest wild woman

We are her new army as sisters of light

As sacred Keepers of Flame

The weavers of myth that keeps hope alive

For our vision, our hearth and our dreams. M.W.

The Lesson:

When the student is called to heart and embraces an act of power, they are then pushed upward to a new ring of power. They can then begin to realize the path of their true destiny.

With the final curtain, the sisters of East and West decided we would hold another family camp. This time, however, our act of power would be huge. We hoped to begin with a cultural exchange. We would have some of the Russian women come to Canada for a visit, and in the summer several of us would travel to Russia for the camp. Remembering our fiery experience, we moved forward from a great call from heart.

An act of power is when you focus your heart energy upon a particular goal. Lynn Andrews wrote extensively about an act of power. It was based on the concept that a student wishing to evolve would move through rings of power (1). Just like the arousal of the fiery heart experienced in the last camp, when one focuses their intent on a goal or act of power, the student can then push through to a new ring of power. Creating this achievement of beauty the student can then begin to understand their true destiny path. (2)

Our collective East-West group consisted of a very small group of women. In Canada it was made up of The Grace Group, a non-profit society. Their goal was to create a global community of women and their families, pursuing cultural exchange in honor of the sacred feminine.

The Grace Group began fundraising and it was their society that would issue invitations to three Russian women. Within any act of power, obstacles occur. First we had challenges around purchasing tickets and then mailing them to Russia. The tickets were sent by courier, and as we tracked their route on the computer, progress suddenly stopped and began moving backwards. It was most bizarre. Knowing the tickets wouldn't arrive in time, we convinced the ticket agency to reissue the tickets, this time to be picked up in Perm. This, of course, was more expensive, but the second issue appeared just hours before the Russian women were to board the train for Moscow to catch the connecting flight to Canada. With the visas already approved the clock was now ticking.

Anna, the young interpreter, got so ill just days before her departure that she was taken to hospital. Despite medical advice to the contrary, she discharged herself, walking home in the freezing cold, determined to be on the train to catch her flight to Canada. Curiously, once on the train her extremely high fever magically disappeared; it became a testament of faith and heart for all sisters concerned.

The Russian women's visit was filled with magic and joy as the connection between East and West blossomed. During their stay, plans were made for summer camp. We would continue along the theme of the new story, but an even greater focus would be on women's unity.

Soon it came time for camp to begin. This year's camp would be held about two hundred miles north of Perm, quite close to Cherdyn. It was situated on a high elevation, looking down over a large valley with a meandering river flowing through it. Facilities were spacious, including facilities for banya. In creating the new story we strove for an atmosphere that would enhance our vibratory energy. As in other camps, we set up a world altar to honor all faiths and traditions, starting each morning with smudging and honoring of the Four Directions, as well as singing Eastern mantras. In addition, this year we also read "The Great Invocation Prayer" by Alice Bailey, which when repeated in Russian is very powerful.

My two young boys that had attended previous camps arrived. So surrounded by light, these two were simply amazing. Over the week of camp I had several occasions to watch one of the young boys as he just very naturally was able to work with energy – at one time bringing the whole circle into calmness. The boys were nine this year.

Since camp was much larger this year, almost one hundred people, and made up mostly of women, it was decided we would have some special women's workshops. Again I would be working with the writings of Helena Roerich. The unity of sisters globally was dear to Helena's heart. In 1930 she wrote to America, stressing this need, and the idea for Altai Sisters and Sisters of the Golden Mountain was formed. Then, the following year there is record of a special correspondence between artist Maria Germanova and the Roerichs (3). Their letters gave us a guideline, a model for the amazing gathering of women at our fourth camp.

In these communications Helena stressed how important it was to reclaim the Feminine Principle, without which there would only be harsh imbalance in the world. She encouraged women to strive for the common good by bringing in beauty – first to their own hearths and then outward to the world. It was to be a message of true knowledge, which could be found in the reverence of spirit and in the openness of our hearts.

Nicholas wrote during this time of a legend that tells of the coming of an era called the Mother of the World; a time, he said, when women would unite and reach new heights. The unity would be based upon life, knowledge, and beauty – the key word being beauty. Of this evolution he said: *"Sisters of the Golden Mountain will speak in the West. Sisters of Altai will speak in Asia...Better than others, the woman knows the element of fire, that element with which is bound the nearest future."* (4)

Our theme, "Creating a New Story," was about moving beyond the old images of jealousy and competition into a place of beauty and celebration, and consequently arousal of the inner fire. In the spirit of celebration we decided to hold a wild women circle, complete with costumes, face paint, and lots of fun and laughter. Flower crowns had been made for the occasion. I began the circle reading some of the quotes from Helena Roerich's writing.

"Strive for knowledge, wisdom and beauty and in the hands of women lies the salvation of humanity."

"Woman is the personification of nature and it is nature that teaches man, not man nature. Women are the guardians of sacred knowledge. Welfare of state rests firmly upon the foundation of family."

"Where women are revered and safeguarded, prosperity reigns and the Gods rejoice."

"The grandeur of the cosmos is built on dual Origin. Is it possible therefore to belittle one Element of it?"

"Woman is the chosen link between the worlds, the visible and the invisible. We must always deepen our knowledge of Mother Nature. Woman must not only defend her own rights but free thought for all of humanity." (5)

After the readings, we began our celebration with drumming and dance. One of the grandmothers arrived late, making a grand entrance dressed entirely in vines and branches, becoming our regal wild woman, Queen of the Forest. It was great fun, and energy was high. We closed the circle with what I call coning. That is, we placed our prayers into the middle of the circle and then, through sound, raised our prayers to spirit. Since we were such a large number, we actually had two circles surrounding the prayers. As our voices lifted up our prayers, the energy in the room was phenomenal! With all good celebrations, we ended the evening with tea and cake. Over tea the Russians sang and taught us the Snake Dance – basically a game where each person joining the snake had to crawl underneath the snakes belly to catch the snake's tail. This amazing energy continued into the night.

Our second women's event was the croning (honoring) of seven grandmothers. Croning, as I've described earlier, is a pagan ceremony that heralds the beginning of the wise-women years. In the past camps we had held ceremonies for mothers and maidens, so it seemed only natural to honor the grandmother. We were croning anyone over fifty, and the eldest participant was sixty-six. Again, as in previous circles, the main part of our ceremony was to form a birth canal for the crones to push through, symbolically miming the birthing of the wise-woman. The grandmothers were adorned, each with a flower crown, and looked especially beautiful. Because of our rather large number the transition through the birth canal seemed incredibly potent.

The final day of camp dawned, amidst much excitement at the prospect of exchanging gifts in this last big celebration. As we gathered for a final time in our huge circle, I looked out at all the shiny, luminous faces full of life and fire, there before me. Camp had become a magnificent experience of true celebration and of living in

196

collaboration with spirit. The great fiery realms had once more guided us to a place of reverence, beauty, and daring – and to joy, doorway to the listening heart!

I sensed this was my final initiation into fire. I could now take what I had learned and move forward. The gifts I had received from fire on this mystical journey had been life changing. The gift of unity between sisters of East and West had been a true gift of spirit, as we stood now united under the banner of beauty. Each of us now stood in a much different place. Standing now as Altai Sisters, Sisters of the Golden Mountain, we had, and continue to make a difference. We can all be the bringers of peace. This ground swell of heart energy coming from this small handful of sisters had brought me to the teachings of fire and for this I would be ever grateful. No national boundaries, no political agenda, just a respect for our diversity, faith in each other, and a willingness to listen from the heart. Imagine!

In the magic of the circle in Shamanic tradition, the circle is closed but always open. Looking back and remembering this heightened energy and its sense of empowerment, as in the wild woman circle, we could each take our experience in creating the new story and continue to move forward. I entreat you to do the same. Call upon the great mythic hero of Russia, the Firebird. Become the hero and embrace the sacred fire within, that divine spark that each of us possess and begin to build your new story. All those many years had been a wonderful journey as I was led along the ancient pathways of

Russia. To paraphrase a statement made by Dominique La Pierre in the *City of Joy*, *"The smiles of my brothers,"* (in this case sisters) *"are lights that will never be extinguished in me."* (6)

Just like the phoenix, the traveller is called to ascend from the ashes and move into the center of heart, move into the energy of fire, this place of passion and true regeneration. Let your imagination take you to new heights and discover your own Zvenigorod, which is different for each of us. Let us move like the Firebird, creating an empowerment which brings forth the radiant truth that we each know in our hearts. Let us all begin to live with the new energies that the Ancient Ones are extending to us for the taking.

May we all begin to build the new story. The opening of the heart becomes fire. Fire then radiates passion and love. After all, love is all there is.

May the journey continue. Ho!

Ancient ceremonial sword

The Lesson:

The final initiation into fire becomes an integration of all initiations. The balancing of the male and female, going back to go forward, ultimately pushing destiny into action.

A year after the camp of 2005, the creation of the new story took a giant step forward. I received word at Christmas that over the summer close to a hundred Russian people from the Perm area had travelled to a place called the Arrows to do sacred fire ceremonies over a period of ten days. They did this in honor of Mother Earth. This area had been chosen because it was a place where three rivers met, a place of the sacred trinity. During these sacred Vedic ceremonies, the bundles that I had shared with the Russian women at the second camp were buried in the earth.

As you may recall, these were bundles symbolizing the ancient days of Atlantis when a high country called Gotl lived by the Feminine Principle in all things. This was based on the temples there of the sun, moon, and the serpent, and were symbolized by string for the hearth, thread for the calling of deity, and knowledge represented by snake. My dear Russian friends had anchored these bundles in Russian soil, anchoring the Feminine Principle in Russia. Just perhaps, these heart centered souls were now opening to choose a higher path.

After the planting of the bundles I felt again as I had at the end of the fourth camp – that my journey had come full circle. Imagine my surprise then, when early in the year of 2008 I received an email from one of the former camp organizers, inviting me once more to collaborate with her in putting on a summer camp in Russia. Keep in mind that there are many different levels of interacting when one moves forward on a Shamanic journey and this would be no exception. On a personal level it seemed that each of us had some shift we needed to make, but as well there also appeared to be a level touching more universal aspects.

Helen, the psychologist who had written me, asked if in addition to the work planned for the upcoming camp, I would also speak about global warming from a Western perspective. She and her team were concerned about the grave ecological conditions in their region. The air pollution in the city was becoming worse and many of the rivers in the area were reaching hazardous levels of pollution. I too had become aware of harsh changes, ranging from species extinction to radical climate change.

James Hansen, chief scientist for NASA, had written an article for *Science* magazine about global warming. In the article he referred to six major tipping points that will occur if we do not take decisive action. An Indian scientist and Nobel Prize winner, Rajendra Pachauri, concurred with this assessment. He stated, "If there is no action before 2012 that's too late. What we do in the next two to three years will determine our future." Helen also made reference to the next forty-eight months, and that at the end of this time there would be a huge shift, the outcome still undetermined.

I had read about the Mayan calendar ending in December 2012 and now needed to explore this whole phenomenon further. Amazingly, what I discovered was that this was also what was called the "end times" for the Cherokee, Aztecs, and the Egyptian stone calendar. I learned too, that Dave Courchene, an Elder of the Anishnabe Nation Eagle clan in Manitoba, Canada had been travelling extensively to light the eighth fire – a ceremony based on an Anishnabe prophecy. This prophecy states:

"They will come to a fork in the road. One road will lead to Materialism and Destruction for almost all living creatures. The other road will lead to a Spiritual Way upon which the Native People will be standing. This path will lead to the lighting of the eighth fire, a period of eternal peace, harmony, and a New Earth where the destruction of the past will be healed."

Was all this just coincidence? Hardly. I continued to explore, turning next to the scientific sector to see what I could learn about the changes with the Earth Herself as connected to this upcoming shift. I came across a website called "weinholds.org" and the enigma of this predicted shift suddenly made sense. Scientists had been monitoring the Earth's electromagnetic structure, and while the electrical field was failing, the magnetic field – what they called Schumann's resonance – was rising. This Schumann's resonance reflects the Earth's heartbeat. The level had already moved from 7.8 Hz. to 9.11 and was expected by 2012 to reach 13 Hz. The frequency of 13 Hz is considered to be the frequency of unconditional love. Simply put, as the planet was moving forward and healing, all things being connected to Her are also healing. Humanity, Earth, sun, the cosmos, all interact. As above, so below and all around… imagine!

Absorbing these profound revelations, I again focused on my preparations for the upcoming camp. My work at all of the camps, although differing slightly in approach, had always focused on moving from the old story of ourselves and embracing a new vision or story. I was about to set out to Russia for the seventh time and this fifth camp would not only embrace stepping into a new story, but would have the added emphasis of creating a story that would help us become impeccable global citizens – citizens that could embrace a life changing shift.

Shortly after arriving in Perm we travelled to a resort outside of the city to begin our camp. With great excitement as to what camp would bring we focused first on releasing the old story. Once exploring the old story we would release it through fire ceremony, but during this process we also went through the processing of healing. This was done primarily through ecstatic trance which I have described previously, but as well we went through a process called a walking meditation. This simply meant stepping back in time to the grandmothers and grandfathers, back through the time lines to learn about patterns that had been set over the generations, often within a fear-based system. During this exercise, as I looked around the room I could see deep healing. Gentle tears flowed down participants faces as they met their ancient ancestors. Given the often harsh history of the Russian people, this healing became both intense and profound.

Camp passed quickly and soon the day of ceremony for the new story arrived. It was to be held on Mary Magdalene's feast day. In honoring spiritual traditions of both East and West, the fire box was prepared in Eastern fashion, encircled by flowers. It was very beautiful and excitement mounted. As each graduate placed their written declaration of stepping into the new story onto the fire, they were gifted with a single red rose in honor of Mary Magdalene.

Heat of fire had fully embraced us throughout our five days of camp, culminating with the birth of each of our new stories. Beauty, reverence, and gratitude touched each of us as together we were able to unite in the place of the fiery heart. Camp ended, as was our tradition, with the ecstatic posture of the Shaman's pose – a posture of celebration. Days at camp had been joyous and full, including a special woman's circle which all had appreciated.

As with other camps, this camp went far beyond our anticipation. We had once more been blessed with the gift of fire; fire around us, even including the appearance of several salamanders – the symbol of fire – for some of the participants. With fire around and within, we each felt the igniting of our hearts with this infinite spark of spirit, helping each and every participant sense the heightened energy of pure grace as we made our shifts to a new story.

Just as I was wondering how we could keep this magnificent momentum of the new story going, the organizers approached me to say they had arranged a surprise. We would be travelling to a small town not far from Perm called Ilinski. Arrangements had been made for me to see an ancient sword housed there in the museum.

The sword, estimated to be one thousand five hundred years old, had been found by a group of anthropologists near Maryanna River at a place where five rivers join. It was a place simply called "the witches place," where old crumbling steps still remained. All eight of the scientists involved in the discovery died – the first of which, upon touching the sword immediately burned up, seemingly like some bizarre self-immolation.

Local folklore surrounding these tragic deaths spoke of an ancient time when women reigned. Historically there were a people called the Chudd from 1000 BC to 6 AD who worshipped the Golden Woman. She was a human size statue representing the Mother of Us All, just like the Turks in Siberia who, in their tradition, called her Om Mai. The statue was made of pure gold and said to have a baby in her belly. This tribe was brutally attacked and all were killed with the exception of one woman who somehow managed to survive. She was believed to have invoked magic within the sword, swearing to kill all men who touched it, thereby avenging her people.

The local Shaman Oleg, however, presented a slightly different perspective. He explained that first of all in ancient times the blacksmiths making these objects possessed special skills, much like alchemists, imbuing the sword with unique attributes. These attributes, combined with the sword's special purpose as a ceremonial sword, made it extremely powerful. This, coupled with the sword lying dormant and hidden for one thousand five hundred years, meant its energy had continued to accumulate, making it both potent and dangerous.

We arrived at the Ilinski museum and the curator explained that being somewhat afraid of the sword the staff had invited two local Shamans to neutralize the power of the sword while unwrapping the sword for our party to see. This ancient old relic sat on a table swaddled in multi-layers of white cloth and intricately tied with red wool. I was invited to examine the sword once unveiled and I gazed down with respect upon this old Ancient One.

It was approximately two and a half to three feet in length, very rusted – having been made of iron – but given its age was surprisingly intact. The hilt of the sword had long since been eroded, leaving only the cross bar where it had once been attached. As I looked down on this ancient artifact I was filled with a feeling of deep reverence for an object that had once been used for these people's sacred ceremonies.

Suddenly I became aware of my whole body heating up. Wave upon wave of heat flashed through my body. My whole body felt like I had been somehow immersed in an overheated sauna. Given my previous initiations into fire where I had also experienced this intense heat, I instinctively knew this sword had belonged to a woman and been used in their ancient fire ceremonies.

Indeed, the Shamans revealed that they believed the sword had belonged to a woman and had been used to call in the Four Directions in sacred circle and also in ceremony with fire. It was also used to remove unwanted entities from the etheric field, somewhat like our present day method of extraction. In their traditions, fire was either in the middle of the circle or surrounding the outer rim of the circle but how the sword was then used they didn't remember. This information had been lost over the course of their long oral history.

The Shamans then told me they had been intuitively aware of my coming and informed me they would also take me to a power spot which was nearby. Driving some distance out of town our group was then directed to walk along a narrow path, walking at times through stands of trees, moving continuously yet gradually upward. Finally we came out into a large open field with a large stand of trees off to one side. Our group was told we must first honor the tribe's sacred tree and were given cookies to use as our offering. Beyond the tree in the open field one could see the faint outline of a circle, still quite distinct despite the overgrowth of vegetation.

I was invited to approach the circle with one of the tribe's women while the Shamans held sacred space for us outside the circle. The woman directed me to a spot on the outer rim of the circle, asking me to use my hand to create a circle of protection around myself. She then invited me to visualize a single heart wish. As I asked the circle to bless these people who were trying to reclaim their ancient tradition I immediately sensed a gentle tugging of my body downward, feeling at once a deep peace and grounding within my total being. Upon completion of the ceremony, both for myself and the rest of my group, we were invited once again to pay a final tribute of thanks to the tribe's sacred tree.

As we made our way back to Ilinski the Shamans told us that this old circle had been used continuously since ancient times. It was a women's circle and was used predominately by older women, the grandmothers. I felt honored indeed to have become a part of their grandmothers' circle. Although their traditions honored both men and women equally, Oleg jokingly told us that in old times when the grandmothers needed to carry out special circles on behalf of the tribe the men were locked up in the village and forbidden to attend. It was an honored role that the grandmothers held, one which brought great wisdom for the tribe.

Contemplating this final initiation to fire with the ancient sword, I sensed a deeper fine tuning of balance – one not previously achieved in the earlier initiations. Upon looking back on the journey, I had first been introduced to fire at the elemental level through lightning, and then gone through the making of the masks to ignite the fire in my blood. From this preparation, plus the further lessons from ancient traditions and the land, I was then able to step into the temple of the fiery heart. This ultimately pushed me, the initiate, into the awareness of destiny. Now, with the masculine attributes of the sword came an awareness of stepping from destiny into action or service. Full circle; full preparations in the lessons of fire.

Alice Bailey, in 1972, wrote of a new group of people who would emerge when needed, and she called them the New World Servers. This group, not affiliated to any one faith, political philosophy or nation, would be connected in the belief of "one." Through an open heart and love of humanity they would wish only to serve, simply following the wisdom of their own souls.

I believe that each of us can move forward to become a New World Server. Using the image of the sword we can step into the place of the warrior. The teachings from the initiation with the ancient sword show that we can cut through distortion and false illusion and begin to see the truth – the real truth. With beauty, as seen through the feminine, we can walk in balance with the masculine image of the sword. Most of all, we can reflect upon the glorious ancient past, learn and move forward. As we cut through that which is false we are also cutting through the veil that separates us from spirit. Fire is the doorway to spirit. The image of the fiery sword can assist us ultimately in moving then to the finely tuned energy of collaboration, both with each other and with spirit.

Action – as the warrior armed with the fiery sword – can bring about change. Chaos theory suggests that even the most minute change sets up mutation and changes the outcome. Clear intention combined with action quite simply brings about change. Shamans have always known this.

These are critical and challenging times. We are continually bombarded with new information that tells us the old story doesn't work any more. Overwhelmed, we are then often pushed to the place of Chicken Little and, believing the sky is falling, becoming afraid and paralyzed. As was once stated, it is the best of times and the worst of times. Take a minute and focus on the best of times and bring forward the image of the ancient fiery sword. In remembering this amazing old sword, imagine holding it aloft and stepping into your role as the warrior, a warrior that carries the vision of beauty and peace. Join the revolution of change – a change filled with the intention of sustainability and respect for all. Take on the fiery power of the old sword, moving forward now into your new story. Together I know we can do it! As above, so below, and all around… IMAGINE!

May the Sisters of the Golden Mountain unite! Ho!

Chapter 23 – Kindello, the Full Round

*Top:
East-West
Sisters*

*Left:
Kindello,
coming full
circle*

The Circle:

Come to the circle, no beginning, no end

Casting the magic, where the dream never ends

Spreading over the web, may the circles now grow.

The Lesson:

A journey moves round in the circle. It is always with no beginning and no end.

Considering the journey always moves in circular fashion, it was then not totally surprising that 2008 would not be the last camp that I would take part in. Spirit had other plans.

At the close of camp in 2008 we travelled back to Perm, preparing for my departure back to Canada. Prior to leaving, however, it was decided that we would hold an open circle for all that had not been able to attend camp. I was delighted to see Milana at the circle. She and I had put on the very first family camp in 2000. She told me that she was now building a permanent campsite and hoped the construction of this site would soon be completed. She invited me to come again to Russia to celebrate the opening of her center.

Life continued on once back home in Canada and soon Russian camps faded back into a distant memory. The New Year dawned, coming with a pleasant surprise. Milana wrote, explaining that the construction of her new center was progressing nicely, and she invited me to come to visit the following summer to take part in her opening.

Upon receiving this good news I wrote back saying I would begin plans to come for the summer of 2010. This would be our sixth family camp and we were once more coming full circle.

As plans moved forward it soon became apparent that preparations seemed fraught with a dichotomy of opposing energies. On one hand there seemed a great push to move towards indeed going back to Russia. On the other hand I was faced with a heavy undercurrent of disconnection and conflict. Woman didn't seem to want to work with each other, while others seemed to have forgotten about my work and were afraid of any mention of Shamanic tradition. It was most disquieting. Again, Anna, the young interpreter, would be coordinating plans between me and the Russian organizers and it seemed we were being pushed into yet another huge act of power.

Despite the challenges, our plans moved forward, and two other women from Canada made plans to travel with me to Russia as well. My focus for this camp would be similar to that of 2008. I would again be helping participants to look at the old story – that place that needed healing. We would then gradually shift the focus to developing a new story – that exquisite place of celebration. This summer I would utilize the use of both ecstatic trance and my guided meditations as the main tools that would assist us in this exercise. We would also do fire ceremonies to augment this practical work. I was excited not only by this upcoming camp, but also to again have the opportunity to see my many friends in the Perm region.

Just prior to leaving for Russia, I got word from Anna informing me that Milana's new center was not ready and we would be holding camp at Kindello instead. This being the location of the first camp, we were indeed moving round the circle – full circle. Amazing!

After our long journey, travelling from Canada to Russia, we finally arrived in Perm and were greeted with great warmth and affection amidst flowers and hearty hugs. It was a joyous reconnection!

This warm reunion was also coupled with concern from the camp organizers. It seemed registration for camp was very low and the organizers were very worried. They had decided to hold an open circle in Perm the following day in hopes that this would help encourage people to come. Overnight a huge shift occurred and soon the numbers of participants had climbed from sixteen to eighty. Remarkable!

Soon we were making our way to camp, meeting yet more families. I would get to see folks I had not seen for two years or more and this would continue throughout our stay at camp. It was one of the highlights of camp for me, as these wonderful reunions continued and I got to see the children – now young adults – having grown up over the decade of my involvement with the camps. Kindello itself seemed unchanged after all these years, with the exception of a new building which now housed a brand new banya. The two camp buildings, located at either end of the camp, were nestled beside the beautiful Sylva River. The river, seemingly untouched by the hands of time, provided the weary traveller with a sense of peace and renewal.

My seminars, or circles, would begin next morning. How does one describe the experience of a circle – especially a circle that would be this large? I remembered a friend that once said it was like trying to describe the experience of first tasting the sweetness of an orange. Until you have had this experience it somewhat remains a mystery. Like the first taste of a juicy orange, stepping into a circle and experiencing the subtle energy experienced in sacred space excites one's soul as it quivers and comes alive, remembering again that true place of home. Camp was like that. Participants felt renewed, slowly coming alive, and they loved it!

The amazing magic and wonder of camp continued each day. I kept wondering, however, about the bigger picture. What did it all mean? Yes, each camp had brought incredible healing and I had learned much at each camp about the otherworldly power of fire. Inwardly, however, I still wondered where it was all leading us.

In the early days of the journey – a journey that now spanned over a period of eleven years – I had been introduced to the prophecies of Edgar Cayce. As you may recall, he had often spoke about the destiny of Russia. He stated several times that "the hope of the world would lie with Russia." (Edgar Cayce Reading #3976-29.) (1)

Early on I was also introduced to the lifetime work of Helena and Nicholas Roerich. Part of this immense body of work they contributed over their lifetime included a quest for world peace, but also a deep-seated central belief that they championed. This central belief that steadfastly remained dear to their hearts was based on an ancient legend. This legend spoke of a time called the Era of the Mother of the World; a time when women would unite. This unity would be based on life, knowledge, and beauty. The Roerichs firmly believed that unity of women around the world would lead to the betterment of humanity.

In 1931, writing to a friend, Nicholas formulated the concept of world unity of sisters. In the West we would be called Sisters of the Golden Mountain and in the East, the Altai Sisters. The Roerichs strongly believed that unity of sisters would enable women to overcome all fiery obstacles. In the unity of women worldwide, we could overcome fear and doubt, ultimately building a true Zvenigorod. This, as you recall, was what they referred to as the mystical City of Bells already existing in the ethers of the upper worlds – a place of peace and harmony. In today's words, with unity we could indeed pave our way to the new story.

Still trying to grasp a clearer overview of the bigger picture I thought also of others who reinforced this belief. Alice Bailey, in her book *The Destiny of Nations*, spoke of Russia having the unique ability of linking East and West. The Maharaji, Baba Virsa Singh, further illuminated the reason behind this ability. He stated simply that Russians do not separate head from heart as is our tendency in the West and are therefore able to grasp the bigger picture.

216

Traditionally, at each camp, as well placing our focus on moving from the old to the new story, we also focused on the empowerment of women. Our sixth camp would be no exception as one evening towards the end of camp we held a women's circle.

The women's circle was very long given the large size of the circle. It was very painful to witness, as many of the women described difficult hardships they were facing daily in their lives. Many of the women in circle seemed a long way from any sense of self empowerment. The circle was both difficult and discouraging.

The next day a shift was about to take place. I was in my room speaking to Olga and Lena, two of the interpreters, discussing the circle of the night before as well as reviewing the day's upcoming activities. The two women began telling me that several of the group leaders who held the afternoon seminars at camp had approached them. Each of these leaders expressed a great interest in beginning women's circles in the near future and hoped they could use my meditations as a part of their circle format.

This news was wonderful and the emotional impact of this hit me like a ton of bricks. I instantly began to cry, feeling a startling *knowing* in my heart center. I now understood why spirit had been pushing me to go back to Perm for this sixth camp. It was all about the coming together of women. This was the birthing of Nicholas and Helena's heart wish – the unity of sisters in Russia.

Over the final days of camp this magical shift continued to evolve. As each of these group leaders came to speak to me, telling me about their wishes and desires to begin women's circles, the foundation of this wish began to take form. Three young people came forward to help me with the logistics of bringing my meditations to Russia. I called this new project The Dakini Project in memory of my beautiful white wolf-dog that had passed away the previous spring.

Anna, my interpreter; Arina, a graphic artist; and Phillip, a sound specialist, were about to help with this first baby step in launching the tapes in Russia. These were young people who had been teenagers when we first began the family camps a decade ago; they were now ready to bring the project into a physical reality. It was wonderful!

The launching of the tapes in Russia would, I hoped, provide ongoing support for forming women's circles in Russia. If we all worked together, just maybe the circles would expand and grow, fulfilling the Reorich's heart wish. It was difficult to contain my excitement, but I took a moment to think back to my early days in Russia. I remembered all of the love and warmth of those memories that still continued to fuel my heart. Teachings I had received over the years had been very simple. The message simply stated: return to heart, return to the sacred, while always remembering to honor Mother Earth. By keeping the fire within always alive, what better way to fulfill this simple message of spirit, but through unity of women through women's circles.

218

I thought back too, to Nadia's dream that she shared with me in those early days. She described how she dreamed that one day the women of the world would come together and encircle the planet in unity. As her dream continued, she saw many, many women standing like a belt around the planet, all of us standing there with our daughters and our granddaughters. She dreamed that we would create a "vibrant living banner." I share Nadia's dream and, like her, I believe dreams are real.

I thought back also to Helena and Nicholas Roerich who shared this same dream. Now their profound heart wish – coming in the form of a birth of the sisterhood, in what they called the Sisters of the Golden Mountain who would come forward in the West, and the Altai sisters in the East – just might take a momentous step forward. Just maybe their heart wish was the fulfillment of Edgar Cayce's prophecy – the hope of the world coming from Russia. Perhaps they were one and the same. I can only hope so.

It is certainly a great beginning. Many spiritual teachers of our day speak of the importance of the return to the feminine. They speak of once more bringing in the balance of feminine energy, now so imperative in meeting the challenges of today's world. They speak also of the need of bringing back a softer, more gentle way of walking on our planet, of bringing back integrity and peace into our world; a true celebration of the new story.

To this end, may the Sisters of the Golden Mountain and the Altai Sisters unite. I believe that if enough of us hold this powerful heart wish, it can and will become a reality. Remember, Nadia reminds us that dreams are real.

So it is above, below and all around. Ho!

Chapter 24 – Destiny

Destiny

Come now to those dear Ones, up there in the sky
In Honor of Mother as we learn how to fly. M.W.

The Lesson:

Around the circle from fire to destiny: reflecting on the lessons from before.

With the final curtain came a time to reflect, having successfully gone through the initiation of fire and achieving unity of East and West. The teachings of fire had indeed been profound. Shamanic tradition is always experiential, and upon looking back, I could not have completed this fiery experience without the sequential levels of the journey.

Step by step, level by level, the Shamanic journey takes us through a wondrous maze of experience that is sometimes painful, more often joyful, provided we can continue to move forward, seeking always to collaborate with spirit. Ever ascending to that inner beauty that each of us possess, and thus gain access to a destiny we never thought possible. Remember, Alice Bailey speaks of this for nations as well as individuals. The individual soul merging with a group soul, always seeking a higher consciousness. Blossoming outward from heart, much like a wildfire that can ignite individuals, then spread out to regions and ultimately fire nations.

Will the Russian people lead the way for other nations and bring the planet to a higher spiritual level? Will they be able to fulfill their destiny as prophecies foretell? Is part of this destiny played out in the building of women's circles, a culmination of the unity of women? I don't know. The experience of my journey in Russia revealed a deeply sacred mystical land, one that I had previously not known existed. Within this mystical enigma were people I had found at a grassroots level that mirrored the consciousness of the land. A fire-filled, heart centered people who strove to live in the new story

222

– the place of *one*. In my trip back to Russia in 2008, I observed a deepening of this spiritual connection, a continuing blossoming of deep faith. The group I had worked with, upon the instructions from their teacher, Muniragi (teaching of Babaji), had been lighting a fire in honor of the Earth every day to assist in the healing and stabilization of their area. I was so inspired by their deep dedication. In 2010 I found people curious and seeking, always trying to follow a higher path. If Russia indeed chooses to follow their destiny, I believe it will give birth from these grassroots people – people choosing to live in the new story. My hope, too, is that each of us will follow the guidance put out like an Earth map for each of our unique destinies as we travel our individual journey of faith.

There is a story told in the magazine *Venture Inward*, called "The Hope of the World," about the August 1991 coup in Russia. This historical event lasted only four days, but within those four days was a single moment when there was a coming together of the "Russian Soul," when "each man (lived) for his fellow man," as Cayce had predicted. (Edgar Cayce Reading #3976-29.) (1)

Ordinary Russian workers stood up against the army and the tanks. Mothers took to the streets, telling the army what was happening and not to fire on their own people. "*Eventually, the Mothers convinced hundreds of soldiers and some tanks to switch sides...The standoff was now grave as brothers lined up against each other. Off in the distance, a small tour boat moved slowly up the river in the pouring rain. Spotting this little tug, someone shouted, 'It's our Aurora!'*"

(The Aurora being a famous battleship that had won a decisive event for the people of the revolution in 1917.) *"Peals of laughter rolled across this conflicted assembly in huge waves...The tide turned at that moment, along with the destiny of the whole of Russia. Laughter bonded brother to brother."* (2)

These people with listening hearts appear to have a collective ancient Russian Soul that is ready to choose a higher path. I have such admiration for the Russian people!

I had first gone to Russia wrapped in the distortions of the old story. Brainwashed since childhood about a Cold War that supposedly existed between the East and the West, and that I should somehow be afraid. Imagine my surprise and delight when the "Cold War" became a distinct thaw as I witnessed my Russian friends greeting me fully from the place of heart.

Our Masters teach us that life experience brings us ultimately to only two choices. We can either ascend or descend. It is that simple, just like the teachings of fire. To ascend we must reclaim wisdom, that true knowledge that comes from spirit and heart. When we descend, we move to a lower vibratory energy embroiled in the fire of conflict. This arena, so filled with hatred, revenge, and addictions, becomes a dismal world of chaos.

By having the courage to step into beauty we take our first baby steps into the fire of pure spirit – home of heart, realm of fiery transmutation. It is then that we discover that Cold War does not

224

exist at the grassroots level. We are just people trying each in our own way to develop the listening heart.

Throughout my decade-long journey, Russia, and Russians, shared with me their ancient heritage, the wisdom of Living Ethics and ultimately the teachings of fire. This amazing experience, often demonstrated in the courageous strength and organizational skills of the Russian women, has taught me that we can break our chains of fear. We can without a doubt move forward and become the new mythmakers. Destiny is that mysterious mystical journey that calls all nations, all men and women of the planet to achieve their calling. If we can catch fire, enliven that spark that lives inside each of us, we can truly create the living magic of a new story.

As a young child I lived in a rural area in Manitoba, Canada. I had never heard of Mary Magdalene and knew little of the vast and beautiful country called Russia. In my early years as an adult I worked in a psychiatric ward, but made plans to leave for the birth of my second child. As a farewell gift my colleagues gave me a book called *Dr Zhivago*.

Almost forty years passed before I travelled to Russia for the first time. It was after this first trip that I began watching the movie based on *Dr Zhivago* each New Year's Eve as a way of renewing my connection to Russia. One day, some seven years later, I picked up my copy of *Dr Zhivago* and took notice of Boris Pasternak's poems at the back of the book. As I quickly scanned through the poems I noticed not one, but two poems dedicated to Mary Magdalene, reminding me of the subtle thread of mystery surrounding the journey. This strange and wonderful series of coincidences did not end there. My Russian friends in Perm then informed me that the village he described in his story was actually Perm. I have since seen the area where Lara's village apartment had once stood.

Imagine my amazement! Imagine a woman called West, and of the West, coming from a simple rural area in central Canada, who was ultimately guided to this very village in Russia – a place in the Urals where the rivers change directions at the point where Europe meets Asia, a place where the River Karma honored me with her point of connection, a doorway where East meets West in the Urals. It is a small world when one is guided by the invisible hand of spirit! Like the great nation of Russia, we each hold in our hands a unique map of destiny that can guide each of us when we open to the fire within.

Step into the arena of the Feminine Principle, a place that is life giving, not life destroying. A place based on creative beauty that can spark the sacred fire in each and every one of us; a place to create the new story, a new myth, for all of our children of tomorrow.

Remember that as we evolve, first we have history, history then becomes legend, and finally it becomes myth. We, dear ones, can be the mythmakers. We are the keepers of the flame; we are the keepers of truth. We are creators of our own reality. We are all the Sisters of the Golden Mountain. When building a myth, one creates something

226

that is always greater than ourselves; myth is stronger than hatred, can even be stronger than love. Like fire, myth lives in our blood. It is the glue that binds us together, which ultimately grounds and connects us to the Earth.

As I transited the path of my fire-filled journey, I met and bonded with many, many sisters. We did find the Golden Mountain and humbly stood at her feet. We are – you are – all Sisters of the Golden Mountain. The choice is yours. To this end, we the sisters of the Earth, encourage and applaud you. We invite you to join now in the greatest myth: to unite in the building of a new time. Ho!

May the Altai and Golden Sisters continue in unity! Ho!

Epilogue

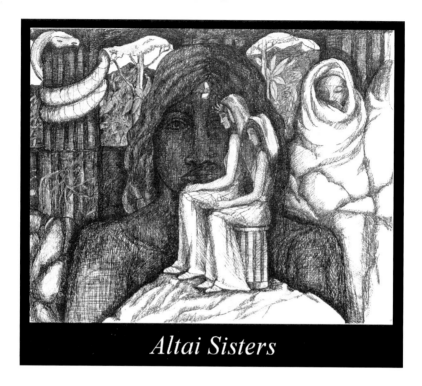

Altai Sisters

"A luminous Woman carries a chalice down from the Mountains. Her face is covered with a veil by Me…A long white scarf is spread down the steps. Female Disciples approach carrying lilies…" (1)

The Invitation:

Come sisters of heart and dear sisters of beauty
We now build a new temple, peace-building our dream. M.W.

From your own place of fire, I invite you, along with the Sisters of the Golden Mountain, to step now into the new story – that place of unity and heart. It is a story based on beauty and the sacred feminine. A way of being that can shift the many challenges we now face in today's world.

Helena and Nicholas Roerich wrote about the Altai and the Golden Sisters. So just who are the Altai and the Golden Sisters? Just like the legends surrounding Shambhala, there are many diverse perspectives. Some believe they are guardians, angelic handmaidens of the Mother of Us All. That is, that they live in the super mundane realms. They are there to help or guide us when direction is needed. Others believe the Altai Sisters to be special beings that walk among us here on Earth. Still others think this name refers to those of us who manage to reach the higher vibratory levels of higher consciousness.

"How should the Altai Sisters be referred to by the people? …Let them be as one to the people." (2)

"But the Altai sisters not only will walk on Earth but also will master many threads of the earthly sphere." (3)

Like the Altai and Golden Sisters, I believe we can all achieve higher vibratory levels. From a place of purity, reverence, and wisdom, we can each bring beauty into our lives and begin this fiery journey to become a Sister of the Golden Mountain. We can unite in the building of the temple called the new story. Can we do it in time?

Let us light the light of new myth and hold this vision as we each build fire and passion in our hearts. Unity is strength as each of us becomes a bold new flower symbolic of spirit knowledge in this new time. As we take on the garment of the pure white lily, we can all step into the Temple of the Sisters of the Golden Mountain and become one. A white scarf is held out, waiting for each new sister in her honor. The pure world of fire is a world of aliveness and beauty, a place of joy. It is that delicate spiral that leads spirit to heart.

Remember that we are, after all, what the Ancients tell us we have all been waiting for. Just like Nadia, we are all dreaming. We can join hands and encircle the planet, our Mother, living out our hopes and our dreams for a new way. Now is a time of celebration, joining the multicolored patchwork of each of our cultures and faiths. It is a time to bring in the resonance of joy, that multifaceted sense of pure essence living in each of us. Imagine our circle now growing, each sister holding the sacred flame in her belly, letting the strength of the flame fan outward, igniting the fire of renewal – renewal in celebration for the planet, bringing forth peace and joy. It can be the weaving of a banner of peace and beauty, creating a circle grounded in the mysteries of the Earth, yet embraced by the splendor of the cosmos.

The music of the flame will heighten, with each of our different rainbow colors blending in the shading of miraculous diverse ethnicity and faith. Within our variegated patchwork will grow a core of harmony and balance. It is a core that is found within the sacred in each of us. A place where the flame will take hold and grow, emanating from a place that is rooted, yet springs forth as a beautiful bloom of promise. A blossom called heart, the home of wisdom for all sisters and brothers.

I can hear the words of a dear sister, "LETS DO IT!"

Across the ancient airwaves the voices of Nicholas and Helena Roerich ring out, as they encourage us all to hold high the banner of beauty, truth, and daring. Listen closely for their words.

"And therefore, I wish you, Sisters of Altai, Sisters of the Golden Mountain, to conquer all fiery obstacles, to reject all fear and doubts – and unwaveringly, untiringly, heroically, patiently build the resplendent Zvenigorod erecting the Indestructible Kremlin of Beauty. And the sighing shall become the inspiration of Benevolence and in the Victory of Spirit shall shine daring and exultation and Beauty. In spirit with you." –Nicholas Roerich (4)

Sisters of the Earth:

Sisters of the Earth are calling to you
Sisters of the Earth are crying for you
Sisters of the Earth are claiming for you
This Mother we call home.

We honor the ones behind us
We honor the ones before us
The stars above and the Earth below
For our Mother we call home.

We are weaving our quilt of stories
Weaving the colors together
And the quilt will girdle the planet
As we call all sisters home.

Each patch holds love and beauty
Each square a heart told story
A garden of truth and beauty
Calling all sisters home.

Sisters of the Earth are calling to you
Sisters of the Earth are crying for you
Sisters of the Earth are claiming for you
Our Mother we call home.

Ho!

Appendix – A History of Nicholas and Helena Roerich. (1)

Included in this appendix is a brief history of a Russian couple named Nicholas and Helena Roerich. Nicholas was a master painter and writer, publishing some thirty volumes of written work and creating over six thousand paintings over his lifetime. Helena was a writer and teacher, who brought us the Agni Yoga Series, Eastern Crossroads, and Foundations of Buddhism. Letters Helena had written to disciples all over the world throughout her lifetime have been published as Letters of Helena Roerich, Volumes 1 and 2.

The Roerichs could be seen as Masters in their own right, totally committed to world peace. They worked tirelessly throughout their lives for the betterment of mankind. Much of their prophetic wisdom lives on today, and the series called Agni Yoga, written by Helena, as inspired by the Ascended Masters, has been distributed worldwide, bringing a wisdom so relevant and essential for today's world.

Nicholas Roerich was born in St Petersburg on October 9, 1874. As a young man Nicholas passed the required entry exams for both the Faculty of Law and The Academy of Arts. His heart's desire, however, was to paint, and it was this path that he followed. He met Helena Shaposhnikova (born February 13, 1879) in the summer of 1900. The couple married on October 28, 1901. They would eventually have two sons, George and Svetaslav.

In 1915, Nicholas became quite ill, so the family left Russia to seek treatment. After his recovery the couple would travel to New York and London. It was in London, in 1920, that the couple made direct contact with the Masters (known as the Mahatmas or Great Souls). This unique connection would continue throughout their lives.

Neither Helena nor Nicholas Roerich were adherents of any one established religion or philosophical movement. Their deeply spiritual philosophy incorporated elements of Buddhism, Hinduism, Pantheism, Theosophy, Russian Orthodoxy, and even the theory of relativity. Out of this eclectic and passionate search for the truth, the idea of an Altai-Himalaya expedition took shape.

In 1925, Nicholas, Helena, and their son George began their Central Asian expedition. This took them through Tibet, across the Himalayan Mountains, into Mongolia, as well as through the Altai Mountains in Siberia. Despite their hardships they all held steadfast to their goals, knowing the journey was a spiritual quest as well as an expedition of scientific research. Nicholas painted hundreds of paintings during their travels.

At the end of the expedition in 1928, the family settled in Kulla Valley nestled in the foothills of the Himalayan Mountains. Here they established the Urusvati Himalayan Research Institute ('Urusvati' is Sanskrit for 'light of the morning star'). Their activities included botanical and ethnological-linguistic studies, collecting medicinal herbs, and the study of ancient medical lore. A laboratory for the study of cancer was installed. The institute collaborated with both European and American Scientific Communities.

Nicholas and Helena worked together in complete harmony in their life work. Their union could best be described as lifelong collaboration in their fields of mutual endeavor. One such endeavor, as seen in Helena's writing, was the destined role of woman in the New Era. (The promotion of women's unity and the forming of The Altai Sisters and The Sisters of the Golden Mountain is found at www.agniyoga.org.)

Perhaps Nicholas's greatest achievement was the development of a Pact for International Protection, both in war and peace, of monuments, institutions, and other cultural treasures. Called the Roerich Pact, its symbol is the Banner of Peace (the Banner of Peace was a symbol consisting of three magenta circles within a circle, on a white field). This Pact was accepted by thirty-six nations and signed by twenty-one. At the time of the signing, President Franklin Roosevelt said, "It possesses a spiritual significance far deeper than the text of the instrument itself." (From The Nicholas Roerich Museum.)

In the late 1940s, the Roerichs decided to return to Russia. Nicholas' health worsened, however, and on December 13, 1947, his heart failed. A large stone was placed at the cremation site in Kulla Valley, honoring a great Master.

Shortly after his death, Helena and George moved to Kalimpong and lived there until Helena's death in 1955. Her ashes were buried on the slope of a mountain and a stupa was erected at the site in her memory.

In India there are two estates which belonged to the Roerich Family – one in Kullu Valley and one in Bangalore. At the time of this writing, the museum in Kulla Valley is under grave threat, the future of this great treasure now uncertain. The house of Svetoslav, in Bangalore, is also not open to the public. The wisdom that Helena and Nicholas brought to the world is an international treasure. Ludmila Shaposhnikova describes Nicholas' work as "bringing us Supreme Beauty." Perhaps the greatest gift from Helena is the message that tells us we can all link up to the virtues of divinity, if we so choose.

May we continue to learn from the profound teachings left by this beautiful couple – a wisdom so needed for this time. Ho!

Notes

Foreword

1. Aum, Agni Yoga, Inc., second printing, 1980.

Introduction

1. The Power of Myth by Bill Moyers and Joeseph Campbell, Doubleday, 1988.

Chapter Three

1. The Animal Style of Perm, 1988.

2. Lost in the Taiga, 1994.

3. Three Remarkable Women by Harold Balyoz, Altai publishing, 1986. (Page 37)

Chapter Four

1. Shakti Woman by Viki Noble, Harper, 1991. (Page 13)

2. Folktales, the majority submitted throughout by Galina Ermolina.

Chapter Five

1. Guidebook, Altai Babas.

2. Ibid.

3. Heart of Asia by Nicholas Roerich, Inner Traditions, 1929. (Page 142)

Chapter Six

1. Edgar Cayce's Story of the Origin and Destiny of Man by Edgar Cayce and Lytle Robinson (Editor), Coward McCann and Georhegan, 1972. (Page 151-152) (Edgar Cayce Reading #3976-29, 1944)

2. Edgar Cayce Predicts – Your Role in Creating the New Age by Mark Thurston, 1981. (Edgar Cayce Reading #3976-10, Feb 8, 1932)

Chapter Seven

1. The Journey to the Center of the Earth by Jules Verne, 1965.

2. The Ancient Wisdom by Annie Besant, Theosophical Publishing House, reprinted, 1918.

3. The Goddess in the Gospels by Margaret Starbird. (Page 8)

Chapter Eight

1. Altai-Himalaya: A Travel Diary by Nicholas Roerich, Aum Press, second printing, 1983.

2. On Eastern Crossroads: Legends and Prophecies of Asia by Helena Roerich (aka Joesephine Saint-Hilaire), second printing, 1992. (Page 62)

3. Return of the Children of the Light by Judith Poich, Linkage Publications, 1999. (page 123)

Chapter Nine

1. Leaves of Morya's Garden, Agni Yoga Inc., Bk2, third printing, 1991.

2. The Collection of the International Centre of the Roerichs, Moscow by Nicholas Roerich, 1997. (Page 12)

Chapter Ten

1. Rainbow Bridge, The Arousal of Fire by Lynn Andrews, 1992.

2. Ibid.

Chapter Eleven

1. Fiery World, vol. 1, Agni Yoga, Inc., third printing, 1982.

2. Ibid.

3. Letters of Helena Roerich, vol. 1-2, by Helena Roerich, Agni Yoga, Inc.

Chapter Twelve

1. The Masters and the Path by C.W. Leadbeater, 1925. (Page 118)

2. Altai-Himalaya: A Travel Diary by Nicholas Roerich, Aum Press, second printing, 1983.

3. Ibid.

Chapter Thirteen

1. Fiery World, vol. 1, Agni Yoga, Inc., third printing, 1982.

2. Rainbow Bridge, The Arousal of Fire by Lynn Andrews, 1992.

3. Shamanic Healing Within the Medicine Wheel by Marie-Lu Lorler, Brotherhood of Life, Inc., 1989.

4. At The Threshold of Two Worlds, Dreams, Visions and Letters of Helena Roerich by Helena Roerich, White Mountain Association, 1998.

Chapter Fourteen

1. Heart, Agni Yoga, Inc., fourth printing, 1982. (Page 199)

2. Ibid. (Page 199-200)

3. Prophecy of the Russian Epic, How the Holy Mountains Released the Mighty Russian Heroes from Their Rocky Caves by Sergi Prokofieff, Temple Lodge, 1993.

4. Ibid.

5. Ibid. (Page 22-23)

Chapter Sixteen

1. Information shared orally by Nicholi Shadowev.

Chapter Seventeen

1. Animal Speak, The Spiritual and Magical Powers of Creatures Great and Small by Ted Andrews, Llewellyn, 1998. (Page 202)

Chapter Eighteen

1. Heart, Agni Yoga, Inc., fourth printing, 1982. (Page 18)

2. Fiery World, vol. 1, Agni Yoga, Inc., third printing, 1982. (Page 7)

3. Fiery World, vol. 3, Agni Yoga, Inc., 1935.

4. Ibid.

5. Edgar Cayce Predicts – Your Role in Creating a New Age by Mark Thurston, 1981. (Page 9) (Edgar Cayce Reading #1602-3, 1939)

6. Fiery World, vol. 3, Agni Yoga, Inc., 1935. (Page 9)

7. Fiery World, vol. 1, Agni Yoga, Inc., third printing, 1982.

8. Serving Humanity by Alice Bailey, 1972.

9. Ibid. (Page 265)

10. Fiery World, vol. 1, Agni Yoga, Inc., third printing, 1982. (Page 13)

11. Letters of Helena Roerich, vol. 1-2 by Helena Roerich, Agni Yoga, Inc.

12. Fiery World, vol. 1, Agni Yoga, Inc., third printing, 1982.

13. Ecstatic Body Postures: An Alternate Reality Workbook by Belinda Gore, 1995. (Page 272)

Chapter Nineteen

1. Folktale, as told by Russian friends.

Chapter Twenty

1. Fiery World, vol. 1, Agni Yoga, Inc., third printing, 1982.

2. The Power of Myth by Bill Moyers and Joeseph Campbell, Doubleday, 1988.

3. Edgar Cayce's Story of the Origin and Destiny of Man by Edgar Cayce and Lytle Robinson (Editor), Coward McCann and Georhegan, 1972. (Edgar Cayce Reading #3976-29, 1944)

4. Destiny of Nations by Alice Bailey, eighth printing, 1990.

5. Black Dawn/Bright Day by Sun Bear and Wabun Wind, 1990. (Page 194)

6. Baba Virsa Singh, including newsletters, News From Gobind Sadan and Godbind Sadan Times.

7. Ibid.

Chapter Twenty-One

1. Rainbow Bridge, Moving Through the Rings of Power by Lynn Andrews, 1992.

2. Ibid.

3. Realm of Light by Nicholas Roerich – www.agniyoga.org

4. Ibid.

5. Letters of Helena Roerich, vol. 1-2, by Helena Roerich, Agni Yoga, Inc.

6. City of Joy by Dominique Lapierre

Chapter Twenty-Three

1. Edgar Cayce's Story of the Origin and Destiny of Man by Edgar Cayce and Lytle Robinson (Editor), Coward McCann and Georhegan, 1972. (Edgar Cayce Reading #3976-29, 1944)

Chapter Twenty-Four

1. Edgar Cayce's Story of the Origin and Destiny of Man by Edgar Cayce and Lytle Robinson (Editor), Coward McCann and Georhegan, 1972. (Edgar Cayce Reading #3976-29, 1944)

2. Venture Inward, The Hope of the World by Shelly Marshall, 1996. (Page 18)

Epilogue

1. At The Threshold of a New World by Helena Roerich. (Page 151)

2. At The Threshold of a New World by Helena Roerich. (Page 88)

3. Ibid. (Page 151)

4. Realm of Light by Nicholas Roerich – www.agniyoga.org

Appendix

1. Original draft by Galina Ermolina, edited and expanded by author, with sources:

a. Jacqueline Decter (with Nicholas Roerich Museum), Inner Traditions, 1989.

b. The Collection of the International Centre of the Roerichs, Moscow by Nicholas Roerish, Preface by Ludmila Shaposhnikova, 1997.

c. Three Remarkable Women by Harold Balyoz, Altai Publisher, 1972.

Textual Sources

Bailey, Alice
–The Destiny of Nations, Lucas Trust, 1949
–Serving Humanity, Lucas Publishing, 1972

Balyoz, Harold
–Three Remarkable Women, Altai Publishers, 1986

Bear, Sun and Wind, Wabun
–Black Dawn/Bright Day, Bear Tribe Publishing, 1990

Besant, Annie
–The Ancient Wisdom, Theosophical Publishing House, 1918

Bloom, William (Editor)
–An Anthology of Essential Writings, Rider, 1991

Cayce, Hugh Lynn
–The Edgar Cayce Reader #2, Paperback Library, 1969

Gorbachev, Mikhael
–Perestroika: New Thinking for Our Country and the World, Harper and Row, 1987

Gore, Belinda
–Ecstatic Body Postures: An Alternative Reality Workbook, Bear and Company, 1995

Lapierre, Dominique
–City of Joy, Warner Books, 1985

Leadbeater, C.W.
–The Masters and the Path, Theosophical Publishing House, 1925

Lorler, Marie-Lu
–Shamanic Healing Within the Medicine Wheel, Brotherhood of Life, Inc., 1989

Polich, Judith Bluestone
–Return of the Children of the Light: Inca and Maya Prophecies for a New World, Linkage Pulications, 1999

Proklfief, Sergi
–Prophecy of the Russian Epic – How the Holy Mountains Released the
Mighty Russian Heroes from Their Rocky Caves, Temple Lodge, 1993

Roerich, Helena
–At the Threshold of the New World, Dreams Visions, And Letters, White
Mountain Education Association, 1998
–Agni Yoga Series, 1924 – 1937
1. Leaves of Morya's Garden 1, 1924
2. Leaves of Morya's Garden 2, 1925
3. New Era Community, 1926
4. Agni Yoga, 1929
5. Infinity, 1930
6. Infinity 2, 1930
7. Hierarchy, 1931
8. Heart, 1932
9. Fiery World 1, 1933
10. Fiery World 2, 1934
11. Fiery World 3, 1935
12. Aum, 1936
13. Brotherhood, 1937
–Letters of Helena Roerich Vol. 1, 1929 – 1938
–Letters of Helena Roerich Vol. 2, 1935 – 1939
–On Eastern Crossroads: Legends and Prophecies of Asia, 1992

Roerich, Nicholas
–Altai-Himalaya: A Travel Diary, Arun Press, 1983
–Shambhala, In Search of the New Era- Inner Traditions, International
Roerich Museum, 1990
–Heart Of Asia – Memoirs from the Himalayas, Inner Traditions
International, 1990 (First published by Roerich Museum Press, 1929)
–Kuluta, International Roerich Trust, 2003
–Realm Of Light, New York, 1931 – www.agniyoga.org

Sams, Jamie and Carson, David (Illustated by Werneke, Angela C.)
–Medicine Cards: The Discovery of Power Through the Ways of Animals,
Bear and Company, 1988

Sarangerel
–Riding Windhorses: A Journey into the Heart of Mongolian Shamanism,
Destiny Books, 2000, © Julie Ann Stewart

Shaposhnikova, Ludmila and Havel, Gerhard
–Nicholas Roerich: Collection of the International Centre of the Roerichs, Moscow, 1997

Starbird, Margaret
–The Goddess in the Gospels; Reclaiming the Sacred Feminine, Bear and Company, 1998
–The Woman with the Alabaster Jar – Mary Magdalene and the Holy Grail, Bear and Company, 1993

Sugrue, Thomas
–The Story of Edgar Cayce, "There is a river," A.R.E. Press Virginia Beach, 1997

Thurston, Mark
–Edgar Casey Predicts: Your Role in Creating a New Age, A.R.E. Press, 1981

Wilkins, Eithne
–The Rose Garden Game, London, 1969

Vasity, Peskov (Translated by M. Schwartz)
–Lost In the Taiga, Doubleday, 1994

Verne, Jules
–A Journey to the Center of the Earth, Scholastic Book Services, 1965

Magazines and Handbooks

Guide Handbook of the Babas, 1997

News from Gobind Sadan, 1995, 1997, 1998

Gobind Sadan Times, Wellwish Publishers, Delhi, 2002, 2004
– www.gobindsadan.org

Venture Inward, The Hope of the World by Shelly Marshall, May-June 1996

Other works by Margaret include:

A Circle of Wisdom: A Journey with the Glastonbury Grandmothers – Capall Bann, 2001

A Journey to Shaman's Rock – CD, co-produced, 2003

Self Published:

Entering the Circle – booklet

Footsteps – A Journey Home to Wholeness, 2004

Guided Meditations – 1988–present (available on website)

Works in Progress:

Dakini the Dancing Wolf (a book about animal teachers)

Imagine – The Celebration of a New Myth.

Read more on Margaret's website:
http://www.margaret-west-connection.com